LEADERSHIP WHACK-A-MOLE

Actionable Strategies for Leadership

Challenges

RIC SHRIVER AND JEFF FIERSTEIN

Leadership Whack-A-Mole

Actionable Strategies for Leadership Challenges

Published by Ric Shriver and Jeff Fierstein
*ISBN: **979-8-9915831-5-2***
*Library of Congress Control Number: **2024912407***

Disclaimer: The authors of this book comment on, compare, and criticize several models and theories generally pertaining to leadership models and practices. The authors are not recommending any particular model or method and any model or method should be implemented with the proper guidance and approval necessary to the situation. The authors' opinions, comments, and criticisms may not be universally applicable to all people in all circumstances. The information provided within this book is for general informational and educational purposes only. Certain case studies and examples are the recollections of the authors that have been recreated from memory and/or supplemented and/or condensed. It is acknowledged that some people may have memories of certain events that differ. The authors make no representations or warranties, express or implied, about the completeness, accuracy, reliability, suitability or availability with respect to the information contained in this book for any purpose. The authors of this book disclaim liability for any loss or damage suffered by any person as a result of the information or content in this book.

For more information, go to the authors' website at www.leadershipwhackamole.com

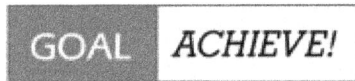

GOAL **ACHIEVE!**

-

Table of Contents

What Readers Are Saying About Leadership Whack-A-Mole

"*Leadership Whack-A-Mole* by Ric Shriver and Jeff Fierstein is more than just a book; it's a blueprint for success and mastering leadership. The back-and-forth banter between these two throughout this book contains relatable and transformative lessons that are pivotal in the journey of growing and retaining top talent in a rapidly evolving world. As a VP of Talent for a boutique technology consultancy, I highly recommend this read to any leader committed to fostering a culture of excellence and driving sustainable growth from within. I found it to be a comprehensive guide that touched upon every crucial aspect of effective leadership, offering profound insights and practical strategies to properly nurture our team's potential.

"Whether it's adapting to shifting market demands, new technologies, or organizational changes, the strategies outlined in this book arm us to handle change with confidence, agility, and finesse."

Ann Berberich

VP of Talent, Paradigm Technology

"*Leadership Whack-A-Mole* isn't just a book—it's a transformative journey through the dynamic world of leadership. Ric and Jeff's bold transparency and personal anecdotes create a compelling narrative that resonates deeply. I applaud Ric's very brave and personal transparency. They don't just talk about leadership; they embody it, sharing real-world examples and actionable insights that challenge you to rethink your approach.

"This isn't your typical leadership manual. Instead of rigid formulas, Ric and Jeff encourage you to embark on your own path, drawing from their experiences to inspire innovation and risk-taking. As you delve into their stories, you'll find yourself reflecting on your own leadership style and strategies for team engagement.

"What sets this book apart is its practicality. It doesn't just theorize; it equips you with tangible tools and approaches that can be applied immediately. Whether you're a seasoned executive or an aspiring leader, the lessons in *Leadership Whack-A-Mole* will empower you to navigate today's rapidly evolving business landscape with confidence.

"More than a guide, this book is a legacy—a resource you'll return to time and again for fresh insights and renewed inspiration. If you're ready to elevate your leadership and make a lasting impact, *Leadership Whack-A-Mole* is your essential companion on your own transformative journey and quest to leave a lasting impact on those leaders you serve."

AlanDial
Founder & CEO, StaffDx

"In their engaging, personal, and eye-opening new book, *Leadership Whack-A-Mole*, Ric Shriver and Jeff Fierstein examine 12 organizational obstacles and, in turn, present new, innovative, and practical leadership solutions for real-world organizational problems. A must-read for all leaders who want to get out of playing "whack-a-mole" and instead maximize their leadership effectiveness. The authors provide valuable insights, innovative strategies, and attainable resources that enable leaders to get to the core of unique organizational challenges. *Leadership Whack-A-Mole* is easy to follow for the novice leader, describes the day-to-day leadership problems, and provides a deeper understanding of effective leadership for all leaders."

Sonja Talley, SPHR/SHRM-SCP

CEO and Founder, CORE HR Solutions, LLC

"Having spent 40+ years working in both for-profit and not-for-profit businesses, I can attest to the significant amount of time and energy that I and other leaders expend in putting out fires and solving workplace challenges. A holistic guide such as *Leadership Whack-a-Mole* would have been an extremely useful tool in helping me develop more positive workplace cultures, better work environments, and higher-performing teams. Exercising my own judgment resulted in trial-and-error approaches that sometimes worked and often did not.

"Ric and Jeff do a superb job of drawing from their own experiences in a humble and sometimes humorous manner to provide practical examples and insights from which leaders at any level can gain insight and knowledge. During my career, I personally benefitted from Jeff's expertise in providing consulting services for two organizations where I worked. I can personally attest to the value that leaders in both organizations received from understanding Jeff's perspectives and implementing his recommendations.

"All leaders possess blind spots and, despite our best intentions, make mistakes. Drawing upon the wisdom and research provided by Ric and Jeff in this book should help equip the reader with new and better tools to develop better-functioning teams and organizations. I thoroughly enjoyed the book and know you will, too."

David H. Richardson, CPA

President and CEO (Retired), Take Charge America, Inc.

"Most readers will go to *Leadership Whack-A-Mole* because they've encountered leadership problems and are in search of practical solutions. That's a wise move because the book is packed with guidance, insights, and checklists, but I'd suggest an additional, more proactive approach: Use this book to evaluate your possible *solutions*, especially the brilliant ones! The authors are frequently asking one of the most important leadership questions of all: And then what? This book can keep your solution from becoming The Next Mole!"

Michael Wade

Execupundit Consulting, LLC and blogger at Execupundit.com

"I've always held the belief that you should treat employees as well as you do your clients/customers. Both are responsible for your success. While you can replace them, don't forget they can replace you as well.

"Ric and Jeff do such a great job on the pitfalls organizations will face if they can't adapt.

"With a large percentage of the workforce jumping ship to join the gig economy, companies risk losing valuable assets if they can't adapt. Unless you're prepared for a completely transactional team, you've got to be open to change.

"Ric and Jeff do a great job of inviting the reader to look through a different lens to identify and overcome challenges. The additional insight from sharing each point of view of the others' experience is really interesting as well."

Angela Moore
President, Six Degrees Digital Media & Founder, The Outsource Authority

"Jeff Fierstein and Ric Shriver have created an essential and timely resource for leaders who strive to develop effective teams with goals and motivations that work together to advance the mission and success of their companies. The book's teaching format encourages thoughtful analysis of each reader's situation to arrive at helpful strategies for managing team growth and effectiveness."

Elizabeth Reich
President and CEO (Retired), Make-A-Wish Arizona

"Ric Shriver and Jeff Fierstein have written a must-read, down-to-earth guide for leaders and HR practitioners navigating today's volatile, complex and increasingly uncertain world of work. Their real, human conversations offer refreshing and transformative approaches which emphasize the critical importance of real-world learning for leaders today. In a world where, as Ric states in the opening, "We are not perfect, nor are the organizations we strive to lead and support," experiential learning and personalized talent development strategies over traditional training are imperative. Why? Because they humanize the learning process and equip leaders and organizations to walk confidently into an uncertain future.

In an increasingly automated and polarized world, the emphasis on human connection and adaptability is not just refreshing but necessary. The vivid examples and clear, actionable strategies make this a must-read for anyone serious about developing authentic leadership skills and overcoming problems that inevitably pop up in our ever-changing world."

Alexa Beavers
Founder & CEO of The Axela Group

Book Overview

What's with the Moles?

Leadership Whack-a-Mole demonstrates the importance of creating and developing flexible and innovative leadership strategies in today's fast-paced business world. We (the authors) humorously use the analogy of "whack-a-mole," the arcade game where a toy mole pops up out of a hole, you hit it back into its hole with a mallet, and another mole pops up from another hole. The object of the game is to keep hitting the moles with your mallet until they all go back into their respective holes. The point is that no matter how many times you whack a mole, another mole pops up. We see the moles as ***problems that keep popping up*** for leaders. We whack them down in hopes of driving them away. But ***another problem pops up*** to take its place. Like whacking the moles in competitive environments, our decisions and actions often have unpredictable outcomes for our businesses. Problems keep popping up, and we find ourselves taking ***piecemeal approaches*** to solve them. Let's fix Marketing. No, let's fix Production. OK, let's fix Engineering. Oh, let's send them to training! Let's buy a new training program. Let's hire another consultant. But nobody is saying, "Let's fix the whole damn thing" by figuring out how to resolve the issues at hand from a ***holistic, organizational systems*** perspective. This book strives to do just that.

Through a career-long personal and professional relationship, we faced nearly every obstacle a leader could experience. The book is built around ongoing conversations between us about twelve leadership obstacles. Through our shared leadership "scenarios," we pose questions designed to inspire readers to examine their own leadership beliefs, values, and the business decisions they make. Each chapter examines how businesses can drive their organizations to success while providing insights, tools, and resources to enable leaders at all levels to maximize their personal effectiveness. Every chapter transitions to the next with a summary of Lessons Learned.

Being a leader is tough!

Authors Ric Shriver and Jeff Fierstein, career business mid-level leaders who are both recently retired, can readily empathize with the millions of leaders who face endless pressures to "perform" in an increasingly competitive, changing, and unpredictable environment. In this book, we engage the readers in a dialogue that will enable leaders at all levels and industries to:

- ➢ *Recognize and understand the unique challenges that leaders face now and into the future.*
- ➢ *Gain further insight and learn innovative strategies to address twelve common hurdles that leaders must overcome.*
- ➢ *Secure access to tools and resources that can enable leaders to address current and anticipated organizational and customer demands in their individual environments.*
- ➢ *Learn how to maximize your leadership effectiveness.*

We have purposely divided the chapters in this book to reflect twelve of the most challenging professional and organizational hurdles leaders experience, the "booby traps" we would have certainly steered clear of had we possessed crystal balls or even "AI" to guide our decision-making. At the start of every chapter, there are "challenge" questions for you to reflect on. These questions help you determine if the insights in the chapter will help you tackle the challenges ahead. Each chapter is structured to reflect the personal experiences we have been through as leaders in (or consultants with) our organizations, followed by key insights. With each challenge, we offer you thoughts, tools, and guidance about how, as a leader, you can successfully navigate your organization's changing landscape. In short, we share our perceptions and experiences for leaders wishing to succeed in the professional, political, power, and organizational challenges life in the business world can present.

The often-painful reality is that our business environments continue to surprise and challenge us by rapidly changing, impacting how we make short- and long-term decisions about our employees, customers, and other stakeholders. Adding to our already "full plates," we continue to see rapidly evolving and ever-increasing demands from the people we recruit, onboard, and develop to serve those customers and stakeholders. Our workforce constantly raises their expectations for us as leaders to create safe, engaging, equitable, and inspiring work environments so they can thrive. Strategic business plans historically developed to execute three-to-five-year roadmaps for success become invalid within six-to-twelve months in some industries, forcing us to constantly retool, refocus, and affect change upon the people, processes, and cultures that maximize performance. In short, our heads are spinning, producing a level of stress and uncertainty that, as human beings, we were not designed or prepared to endure.

The book is not intended to be a "scientific, research-based dissertation," nor do we pretend to be coronated "experts" in the fields of personal and organizational psychology. However, what we believe and share is that leaders would like to see themselves as "high performers," able to make positive, value-added contributions to their organizations. Leaders must employ innovative approaches to successfully navigate their situations. The personal and professional experiences and insights we share in this book will help you do just that.

We will introduce ourselves and share our perspectives on our careers and business experiences. "Scenarios" from our experience are integrated into each of the twelve chapters. We present the scenarios as a dialogue between the two of us, with Jeff serving primarily in a consulting role and Ric expounding on many of his personal or observed scenarios. The twelve challenges are outlined in the previous table of contents.

The good news is that our careers survived the challenges and obstacles outlined in the book, and today, we are able to reflect - with gratification - on the lessons learned and shared in the many global organizations we have served.

Introduction to the Authors:

Our Stories

Ric Shriver's Story

WOODSTOCK, GEORGIA... RIC'S CRY FOR HELP!

"Where is the joy?" I asked with my head bowed as I sat on the edge of my bed, reaching for the buzzing alarm, which painfully reminded me that, once again, it was 5:30 AM and time to prepare for another physically, mentally, and emotionally grueling workday. It was a cold, early February morning in the northern suburbs of Atlanta, and it happened to be my 43rd birthday. After shutting off the alarm, I grew somber, dwelling on the certainty that I had at least another 22 years of enduring this routine. My frame of mind was not consistent with what I aspired to be as a leader, husband, father, son, and friend. By 6:15 AM, I needed to be out the door and on my way into the 8-lane, I-575, I-75, and I-285 one-hour "concrete dogfight" en route to my office. Arriving in my office with my blood pressure soaring, my pulse pounding, and sweaty palms from the freeway malaise, I reluctantly prepared my mind and emotions to deal with continuing employee relations issues, internal conflicts, endless unproductive meetings, and a nagging perception that I could never "measure up" to the increasing demands and expectations of the people I served.

27 YEARS LATER

For many years following that cold February 1996 morning, I continued to struggle with personal and career directions that conflicted with each other. This cost me and countless others emotional and financial strife that has only recently subsided and given way to a greater sense of personal peace and joy that eluded me for over three decades.

From a career perspective, I rose to an executive-level role within a year from that morning. I eventually transitioned into a similar role in a rapidly expanding start-up contract services company, moved into a senior executive role with a national sub-contractor to the healthcare industry, and then ultimately assumed an executive role for the largest division of a national, for-profit enterprise with the responsibility for Human Resources and Organizational Development functions supporting 25 facilities and over 22,000 employees.

The career progression came with significant personal costs – two failed marriages, a debilitating lower back injury, significant weight gain, high blood pressure, and personal health habits that, by early 2013, were spinning out of control. Significant income gains and travel came with the career progression – typically, 70 to 80 percent of the time was spent on the road and in the air, leaving little time for living my "best life!" For those of you who have experienced chronic physical pain along with the increasing demands of a career and a turbulent personal life, you are no doubt getting a clear picture of the stress level I was enduring. Looking back on those years and the trials they presented, I can attribute much of my disappointment to my own personal choices and to the organizational cultures and decision-making I was exposed to.

Fortunately, I have maintained a long-term friendship with Jeff Fierstein, the book's co-author. Jeff and I began working together at the corporate headquarters of a national healthcare company, and ultimately, I wound up reporting to Jeff. After just a few short years, and before the infamous February morning I referred to earlier, Jeff and I became the victims of a corporate downsizing because of restructuring. We agreed to stay in touch. We even had the opportunity to work together on a couple of short-term consulting assignments in the early 90s. Then, in the late 90s, I hired Jeff as a mid-level leader reporting to me! That working relationship lasted until the national contract services company we worked with was sold to another, larger international company. Once again, we were both back in the independent consulting business. Within a short time, we found ourselves once again in separate corporate environments. We faced cultural and political obstacles that hindered our efforts to make a meaningful impact on many of the companies we worked with. With occasional visits and frequent phone calls, we kept our sanity intact by talking about our experiences.

As we embark upon describing our own experiences over the past four decades, I am reminded of the words of wisdom Jeff imparted to me during the period I was reporting to him in the 80s. While complaining to him one afternoon about the behavior of a couple of our senior leaders in a recent meeting, Jeff straightforwardly (and facetiously) told me, "Ric, your job is to sit there and let other leaders throw shit at you – if you get hit, you get paid. If you duck, you get yelled at. And, God forbid, if you throw the shit back at them, you get fired!" Throughout the years, I thought he was joking. Unfortunately, in many of our organizations and through many challenging experiences, I have learned that he was telling me the truth!

I close my story with words of wisdom to help keep your focus on your career and life in proper perspective: "Life is difficult." That is the opening sentence in one of my favorite books, *The Road Less Traveled* (1978), by Scott Peck, a Christian Psychologist who provided some keen insights in his book (and other books he authored) about the challenges we face in our personal and professional lives. Each day brings a new set of obstacles for us to face. As Jeff and I reflect on our careers and the organizational challenges we faced, we are reminded of our human fallibility. We are not perfect, nor are the organizations we strive to lead and support. We do our best to confront the hurdles before us, recognizing that our world will continue to change. With the changes in our internal and external environments will come new headwinds, forces that will compel us to confront and ultimately overcome those challenges.

I hope that you can identify with the many trials a typical leader faces and how, from our lessons learned, you might better navigate similar trials. Our goal is that you will review the experiences outlined in this book to nurture a work environment that forms a greater sense of dedication for, and engagement and alignment with, your entire organization.

Jeff Fierstein's Story

PHOENIX, ARIZONA... NO MORE FLAVOR OF THE MONTH PROGRAMS

Wow! What a journey! As an internal and external Management/ Organization Development consultant, I've seen the "flavor-of-the-month" interventions for over 40 years. In my career, I learned quickly that public and private organizations are highly complex and static entities that are challenging to manage, let alone change. I've studied strategy, execution, systems, culture, productivity, processes, quality, and the rest, looking for the answers to my clients' business problems and improvements. However, I learned that one cannot find the answers in a one-shot program dealing with one segment of the organization. Flavor-of-the-Month (F.O.T.M.) programs cannot create sustained large-scale change because the segmented issues or performance problems are part of a larger, more complex "system." As we know from Open Systems theory, once we change one part of the system, it affects other parts. As we'll discuss later in the book, often segmental change "suboptimizes" parts of - or the entire - organization.

So, I spent years struggling with individual F.O.T.M. programs and interventions, knowing full well that they would die quick (or not so quick) deaths as most do. It has been a frustrating experience trying to convince leadership and clients that there are better ways to solve their problems and grow their companies. I've spent most of my career as an external consultant because I found that internal consultants are too often a part of the F.O.T.M. dynamic. Like my friend Ric, I encountered resistance and resentment from clients, bosses, and peers for going against the F.O.T.M. grain. I ended jobs and projects because I "threw the shit back" (as I counseled Ric not to do many years ago) in advising my clients against quick fixes in the form of F.O.T.M. programs. That was neither my goal nor consistent with my values. I wanted to help businesses (I'll use this as a generic term for profit, non-profit, and government organizations) fix their problems, grow their businesses, and build cultures that respect people and their work. And I wanted to do it from a "systems" approach.

When I taught graduate-level Organization Development (OD) classes at a university, I explained to my students that OD was not segmented interventions but a holistic systems process – not a piecemeal approach. Over the years, I watched the "functions" of OD change with the F.O.T.M. winds. This year, virtual training; next year, succession planning, then team building, Total Quality Management, personality profiles, 360-degree assessments, performance reviews, talent development, and so on. At the start of my OD foundation class, when I asked my students to define "individual development" in the workplace, they immediately and consistently said that it was developing a person for new skill acquisition, performance improvement, career development, replacement, or succession. The focus was always on "a" person. So, it was with their definition of "team development" – assessment, planning, and activities/programs to develop or fix a team. My students, however, could not grasp the concept of "organization development;" that is, they could not see how one could "develop" an organization. My students' experiences in business were watching management gamble on F.O.T.M. programs – even when those efforts didn't work as hoped.

Ric and I have spent years discussing the failures and limitations of segmented interventions in business (even working together on some). The companies we worked for – individually and together –

were looking for quick fixes to discreet, albeit large, problems and needs. This book shares what we have learned (and felt) in trying to apply a sensible systems approach to developing organizations and to the barriers and resistance we've encountered. We hope this will be helpful to you on your journey to lead and improve your business as well.

Still, we have a crisis looming in American business today. We see significant changes in global and domestic economies, geopolitics, pandemics, market turmoil, energy, workforce and workplace changes, technology, etc. The chaotic "digital" age is upon us, yet leadership in our organizations continues to lead with Industrial Age practices and mindsets. Look at the outdated practices embedded in our businesses today: working in the office, annual employee performance appraisals, centralized, top-down decision-making, rigidity in organizational structure and design, rigid job descriptions that stymie workers' growth and job satisfaction, and so on. American business is still going through an evolution from the Industrial Age to the Information Age work. The massive knowledge explosion, the introduction of new technologies, and a dramatic shift from industrial to information jobs cause pain as we figure out how to adapt to a new world of work. Now, we are evolving from the Information Age to the Digital Age and adapting to the enormous changes we see today – and will continue to see for many years. In the words attributed to the ancient philosopher Heraclitus, "change is the only constant in life."

We are only now adapting to the new Digital Age as we encounter yet the next "age." We must become highly agile with a constant mindset of change. We will take note of the ideas of futurists showing us the next paradigm shift and begin our evolution into the next era of work. Ric and I see this book as more than just the state of leadership today. We augment every chapter with well-rounded thoughts about our collective journey into the future of leadership and organizations. We want you to be as forward-thinking as we think this book is and gain ideas to help you and your business transform today and into the future.

Chapter 1

Becoming a Leader–What Now?

The Moles are Problems and Challenges to Overcome

CHALLENGE QUESTIONS FOR THE READER:

1. What would you say makes a great leader?

2. What are your beliefs and values, and how do they influence your leadership style?
3. How do you define "leadership?"
4. What is your leadership style? Is it effective in your current environment and culture?
5. What leadership skills and abilities do you need to develop to prepare your organization for changes coming?

LEADERSHIP WHACK-A-MOLE

RIC'S INTRODUCTION TO LEADERSHIP

Most leaders I have had the pleasure of working with have followed a similar and all too common career path - they excelled as individual contributors/professionals in the early stages of their careers. Because of their competence, adherence to corporate values, and ability to meet behavioral expectations, they were promoted into formal leadership roles, typically without formal preparation! Like me, they most likely asked, "What is a leader?" and "What should I now be doing differently?"

Our definition of a leader is someone who leads individuals and other leaders toward desired outcomes. A formal definition of a leader is "a person who builds and maintains a team that performs well relative to its competition" (Hogan et al., 2018). In short, a leader establishes a vision, aligns resources, and achieves results. That sounds like a simple formula for success, right? Then why have so many of us struggled throughout our careers, trying to make these three things happen regularly and consistently?

Early in my "leadership" career, I managed the day-to-day operation of a "Personnel" department in a not-for-profit organization employing 2,000 people. Because I had previously assumed formal leadership responsibility as a Petty Officer in the U.S. Navy, the concept of providing oversight and supervision to a team of people seemed manageable. The scenario I describe below shows just how ill-equipped I was to lead a team of challenging individuals.

As an inexperienced 24-year-old, I found myself in my first leadership position as the "Assistant Personnel Director" for a department of seven individuals, most of whom were older than me.

LEADERSHIP WHACK-A-MOLE

With my military background, I felt confident that leading the people in the department would come naturally. That was not the case! The staff drove me crazy! My job required me to handle data, listen to employee complaints, and manage internal processes. The staff in the office frequently displayed outbursts of laughter, gossip, and other annoying distractions, which were getting the best of me. One nerve-racking day, when my emotions were already wound up like a top, their constant chatter pushed me to my limit. I got out of my chair, moved to my office door, and, with a loud voice, asked them to please be quiet. My controlled display of emotion didn't seem out of line–I had experienced similar "leader interventions" from my superiors while serving in the Navy.

The Personnel Department in Roanoke, Virginia, was a long way from North Africa, and my maturity level as a leader was a long way from where it needed to be! The people I supervised judged successful leaders based on their ability to collaborate, communicate, be flexible, and resolve conflicts effectively. This expectation certainly differed from the military's "command-and-control" style of leadership, which I had been accustomed to.

As I continued to lead the staff in the Personnel Department, team members grew more resentful, distrustful, and disengaged. At the ripe old age of 26, I was failing as a leader, and I instinctively knew it. Swallowing my pride, I finally returned to graduate school to pursue an MBA, hoping to shore up my credentials and ability to be a better leader.

While pursuing my graduate degree, what I quickly grasped was the importance of careful and thoughtful planning for any leader aspiring to achieve positive results with their teams and for the organization. Besides creating thorough and carefully prepared short- and long-term plans, it is crucial for the leader to comprehend the internal and external environments they operate in. This involves constantly evaluating and adapting to the organization's culture, marketplace, and socio-economic shifts, which influences both business and personal outcomes for leaders in all kinds of enterprises.

Those internal and external changes require leaders to adjust and adapt well-crafted plans to achieve desired outcomes. An analogy that we can understand and appreciate is the comparison of our assumed (or assigned) projects to the "flight plans" airline pilots must always have before "pushing out" from the gate. The flight plan defines the aircraft's path to a confirmed destination. That "path" will include such factors as the altitude, timing, pilot, first officer, and flight crew expectations and roles. Seasoned and intellectually capable pilots will always be aware of the changes that, without exception, arise during the flight.

A classic example of how being closed off to the vulnerability of supportive technology, human error, and altered external circumstances can result in disaster is the story of American Airlines Flight 965 in December 1995 (Green Dot Aviation, YouTube video). The Boeing 757-200 was en route from Miami, Florida, to Cali, Columbia, with 159 passengers on board. The crew had meticulously followed all the elements of the flight plan as the plane's captain firmly believed in following the plan exactly as prescribed. Unfortunately, on this flight, the captain, to save some previously lost time, decided while descending into Cali to "take a shortcut" and override the original flight plan, which had been prepared to enable a safe path through the mountains surrounding the city. That decision compelled both the pilot and the first officer to expedite preparations for the landing, adding unplanned stress and distraction in the cockpit. That decision, coupled with a lack of sophisticated ground and air traffic control technology in Cali, caused the pilots to turn the plane in the wrong direction during their descent. The captain and first officer, during their hasty actions to alter the course of the flight, were unaware that the navigation system had not been reprogrammed properly-there were no warning lights or other alarms to indicate that there might be a problem with the coordinates being reported by the navigation system. However, as the aircraft descended into Cali, the first officer noticed that some of the expected landmarks were not visible on a clear, high-visibility evening. The first officer questioned the captain about the exact location of the plane and challenged the captain to return to a higher, safer altitude above the peaks of the nearby mountains to verify their exact location. The captain, being a strong advocate of always "sticking with" a plan (even an altered one) and feeling confident because of his previous experience flying into Cali, chose to ignore the advice of his first officer, made an incorrect turn, and continued the descent and approach as prescribed by the updated flight plan. The blind adherence to the plan the captain chose to pursue ultimately led to an unplanned rendezvous with a nearby mountaintop, resulting in the deaths of 155 of the 159 souls on board.

The tragedy of Flight 965 reflects a rigid leadership mindset that too often creates dysfunction and undesired outcomes for our teams and companies. Flight 965 and another previous Eastern Airlines crash in South Florida caused the Air National Transportation Board to impose a new set of cockpit guidelines for crew behavior called "*Crew Resource Management.*" The guidelines compel all crew members to understand their respective roles and responsibilities and the requirement to "speak up" when something is not right with the flight. These new guidelines are emphatic about expecting captains to be open to potentially contradictory perspectives of the other members of the flight crew and to avoid dogmatic, authoritative responses to input and advice from crew members.

How often have we seen teams and organizations derail in their efforts to improve because the leaders are obsessed with power, ego, "shiny new object" distractions, impulsive and impatient decision-making, or close-mindedness? The inability of both leaders and members of our teams to openly communicate with each other about all the factors that must be considered too often keeps us from being individually and organizationally successful. Rigid, overly complex job descriptions contradict the need for individuals with complementary skills to openly collaborate, communicate, and accurately respond to the rapidly changing environments they are working in, i.e., "individuals can't see the forest because of their focus on the trees!"

The many circumstances leaders must constantly respond to and work through reinforce the reality that being a leader is demanding, challenging, and difficult. I often believe that effective leadership is more than a science; it is also an art that must be continuously refined to maximize the positive impact we aspire to achieve in our leadership roles.

JEFF'S RESPONSE TO RIC'S INTRODUCTION TO LEADERSHIP

Leadership is a tricky concept to define. Management guru Warren Bennis (1997) purportedly identified about 850 definitions for the term. Hundreds more surely have developed since then. We have had the great man theory, transformational leadership, servant leadership, situational leadership, visionary leadership, purposeful leadership, command and control leadership, agile leadership, authentic leadership, remote leadership, etc. Given the multitude of leadership styles and definitions, how can we find leadership's true essence? Ric gave a general definition of leadership, stating that it establishes a clear vision and expectations for outcomes, creates alignment with resources, and ensures that results are produced. It sounds simplistic. And it is, in theory. However, leading an organization, a department, a team, or any business or non-business entity is a complex undertaking that embodies a set of beliefs and supporting behaviors by the leader.

Here are my thoughts about what makes an effective leader:

It depends! What is the environment in which the organization is working? An effective leader in one situation may be a disastrous leader in another. Here's an example: John is an experienced social work mentor. His effectiveness in his role stems partly from his temperament and belief in assisting other experienced social workers. In his approach to mentoring, John uses a non-directive style. He asks rather than tells. Now, let's switch John's role. He is a Marine boot camp drill instructor. How does his leadership style transfer to his new role? Most likely, it will not make him an effective drill instructor – a leader of men and women being trained to fight the enemy (among other "job duties"). Successful leaders have traits in common, but their effectiveness varies depending on the situation.

A successful leader chooses the best leadership style for the team's "development" level. For example, a team with little skill or experience in a particular job would be led in a more "commanding" style. In contrast, another team that is experienced and performs more independently would be best led in a "laissez-faire" (hands-off) leadership style. For example, our Marine drill instructor will exhibit a commanding leadership style because of the group's "low" development level and the hierarchical nature of the organization. Our social work mentor, working with highly developed social workers, will take a more hands-off approach. As the Marine recruits "develop" in their "jobs"- becoming more proficient - leaders would change their style to fit that higher "development" level. In this model, being an effective leader depends on adjusting to the development level of the people you're leading and the culture you're in.

Beliefs, values, and personalities also affect a leader's style and performance. Ric's description of the American Airlines tragedy shows the underlying beliefs and values of a captain who followed the rules so narrowly that he would not listen to the first officer, resulting in an unfortunate crash. I've worked with leaders who believe new employees should "figure out" how to do their jobs and the performance standards that go with it, unlike leaders who believe new employees need training and guidance. Some leaders value employees "staying until the work is done," as opposed to others who value a 9 to 5 work schedule for work-life balance. Some leaders prefer a micromanaged approach, while others prefer a hands-off approach. As a note, these styles fit into a situational leadership model. As a highly "commanding" manager, I was not especially effective in hiring teams with "high development" who required a hands-off approach. Instead, I was always "looking over their shoulders." Was this my personality in action? Without a doubt, it was. Might I have been better suited as a drill instructor? Through my upbringing, I incorporated certain beliefs and values about people and work that directly affected my leadership style and effectiveness.

LEADERSHIP WHACK-A-MOLE

We spend much time and money trying to change leaders' behaviors to make them more effective (called "leadership development"), but that is often difficult. Instead of promoting the best technical specialists, we should consider "personality" (values, beliefs, and traits) when considering people for leadership positions. Adizes' *Corporate Lifecycle* (1989) and *Griener's Growth Model* (1998) demonstrate that a leader must adapt to an organization's changing growth stages to be effective. In the early stages of a business, a leader uses entrepreneurial beliefs and behaviors to achieve success, focusing on sales and adaptability. With the organization's growth and increased complexity, the leader needs to develop new skills and behaviors in managing and growing operations. This explains why "professional managers" sometimes replace entrepreneurial company founders.

Ric's experience as a leader in his early career showcases how personality impacts leadership. He talks about the office disruptions that the staff created and his response to them. Ric's beliefs about managing people (as learned in a military setting) influenced his thinking and behavior as a leader. Knowing Ric as I have for 40 years, he worked diligently to overcome his earlier beliefs about how to lead and manage people.

Think about the people who have not overcome their biases, prejudices, and strong beliefs as they become leaders. This explains why micromanagers struggle with employees who are in a remote work setting. What are your beliefs and values, and how do they influence your leadership style? The next chapter will examine how a leader develops–what works and what doesn't!

Decades of research show us what the future looks like for enterprise leaders. Chaotic changes in the company's markets and the environment are redefining the role of senior leaders. The Industrial Age leader will no longer be the charismatic, visionary "top dog" who controls the overall work and output of the organization. Leaders will facilitate the company's adaptation to change in harmony with the business strategy, culture, and goals. Empowerment will flow throughout the organization to better exceed customer expectations, improve productivity, and stimulate strategic innovation. Leaders will direct downward communication to all employees, enabling them to align their work, projects, and career progression with the expected company strategy and outcomes. This will go together with decentralized power and decision-making. The future leader model requires senior leaders with different beliefs and behaviors than what they currently have in their "command and control" roles. Leadership development will be necessary to help these leaders improve their skills and practices. This may require coaching from outside experts. For those senior leaders who cannot make the changes, a replacement for their positions may be necessary. Developing lower-level leaders can build the "talent bench" for future senior leadership roles.

The role change for senior leaders will, by necessity, change the role of mid-level leaders. The Industrial Age manager's role was to control work output by organizing and directing the tasks of the workers. Henri Fayol's book *General and Industrial Management* (1949) listed the following functions of management: planning, organizing, commanding, coordinating, and controlling. For most of the 20th century, this was the template for the manager's role. It still is (see any current management textbook), even today. Most managers work in organizations where senior leaders and the company culture expect, design, and reinforce these traditional roles.

LEADERSHIP WHACK-A-MOLE

The future mid-level leader helps employees grow their skills, collaborate effectively, and advance in their careers. This will require skills that managers lack today, in part because their leaders have neglected them in **their** development. Just as employees will need "reskilling," so will their managers. Managers must become proficient coaches who guide employees in the tasks cited above. They will coach employees to work effectively in project teams–especially cross-functional ones. They must let go of the "control" role, which will be difficult for many managers. Employee work will expand from functional to strategic, with the manager guiding the expansion. As companies shift toward a skill-based approach, hiring workers will be an unfamiliar task for managers. They will focus less on formal education and specific job roles. Managers will need new skills in recruiting and selection, including the ability to determine a candidate's future potential in the company and a general capability to develop into more strategic roles in the business.

Middle managers will need to think strategically as the linchpin between senior management and employees to carry out work aligned with the company's goals/priorities, performance demands, and culture. Managers will focus more on "soft skills" like coaching, communication, and emotional intelligence to excel in their new roles. Remote team management is rapidly becoming a required skill set for managers to coordinate virtual work with workers. Team skills will still be necessary; however, employees will experience their "team" in various project and innovation teams they serve on, not only in their functional ones. During the performance appraisal process, we will gather feedback from various team members and managers who collaborate with the employees. This will involve working with other managers, project leaders, and team members, so they'll need networking skills and the ability to gather information. The manager will assist their employees in performing effectively in networks and project teams, perform their "job description" duties well, and plan and develop strategic skills for the future. Collaboration skills will be critical for working with various teams, cross-functional managers, and employees.

In the past, top leaders considered middle managers dispensable when company performance declined or when customer, market, or environmental changes unintentionally affected profitability. Self-managed teams became popular in the 1980s and 1990s, at which point management theorists predicted the demise of middle management. While some companies eliminated management positions, most kept the same organizational structures. Middle managers will be even more important in the new era of management to ensure successful organizational changes. The imperative is clear – we must place a high priority on the continued development of leaders at all levels, particularly at the mid-level! We will focus on the best ways to develop our leadership skills in the next chapter.

LESSONS LEARNED

Becoming a Leader–What Now?

1. A simple definition: Leaders establish a vision, align resources, and achieve results.
2. There are about 1,000 definitions of leadership.
3. We need to know ourselves to be an effective leader.
4. Leadership is situational and depends on the culture of the organization and the development levels of the followers.
5. One's beliefs, values, and personality affect a leader's style and behavior.
6. Leaders' behaviors and styles must change with new stages of the organization's growth.
7. Markets and environments are changing, and so must leaders' skills and abilities.
8. Middle managers will become the critical linchpin between the organization's strategies, vision, culture, and goals and project and functional teams.

LEADERSHIP WHACK-A-MOLE

***

Chapter 2

Leadership Development - Becoming an Effective Leader

Learning to Whack the Moles with Finesse

CHALLENGE QUESTIONS FOR THE READER:

1. What method(s) do you use to determine current leadership competencies in your organization? Your future competencies?
2. What methods do you use to train and develop current and upcoming leaders? How effective are the methods?
3. How much money does your business spend on leadership development? What is your return-on-investment?
4. Does your organization allow developing leaders to make mistakes and learn from them?
5. Is your leadership training more information dissemination or experiential and applied on the job?

LEADERSHIP WHACK-A-MOLE

RIC'S QUEST FOR LEADERSHIP EFFECTIVENESS

I recall a discussion with a senior HR leader a few years ago regarding their perception of how leadership competencies should be prioritized, evaluated, and developed for our organization. They answered, "We'll just pull some respected leaders into a room, serve them refreshments, and hammer the leadership competencies out!" I then asked if the identified competencies should apply to every leader at every level, and the response was a resounding "Absolutely." I scratched my head at the response, wondering how accountability for learning, performance, and organizational impact could be measured. What we intend to do in this chapter is outline some practical and, most importantly, effective ways to enhance our leadership knowledge, skills, and abilities with the ultimate goal of positively impacting business results.

Over the past couple of years, I have partnered with a publishing and consulting firm called TalentTelligent™. The firm's founders, Roger Pearman, Ed.D., and Robert Eichinger, Ph.D., have used decades of research and experience to create "performance libraries" that consider the unique roles, responsibilities, and practices needed to be effective as a leader, manager/supervisor, and individual contributor. They have proven that our business environments are different and require unique talent management approaches. The established libraries are built on 50 years of extensive research with global organizations and through their work at the Center for Creative Leadership, a well-recognized "gold standard" for leader and professional development. The underlying belief of TalentTelligent™ is that every organization must regularly assess - for leaders, managers, and individual contributors - what the most important roles, responsibilities, and behavioral best practices have the most significant impact on the individual's ability to be successful within their positions. They introduced a digital card-sorting process that calls for selected groups of leaders, managers, and individual contributors to collectively identify what roles, responsibilities, and supporting practices should be prioritized and developed in support of the business goals and priorities. The resulting framework, tailored to the enterprise at each stage of the organization's evolution, enables the client to use custom TalentTelligent™ tools and resources to select the best-qualified individuals for every role in the business, regularly assess the performance of every individual leader, manager, and contributor, and provide a development platform they call "Develop-It-Yourself" Digital for targeted development.

What is particularly unique about the TalentTelligent™ framework is that it is on the leading edge of using "generative AI," defined here as "Authentic Intelligence," that enables employees to construct and implement individual development plans based on asking questions in their own words using the AI Chat-based feature. Dr. Eichinger (as a member of the team that advanced the "70-20-10" theory of development (Pedler, 1997) at the Center for Creative Leadership), purports that most individual development recommendations focus on the learner's responsibility to engage in "experiential" learning under an accountable coach's supervision and mentoring. While online visual and written resources are included in every individual development plan, the emphasis on individual development can focus primarily on experiential learning.

The TalentTelligent™ framework defies the logic behind spending $166 billion (Westfall, 2019) in a leadership development industry that many organizations have fallen prey to. Often, well-designed, visually attractive "training packages" are sold to businesses with the idea that massive "deployment" of these packages will alter the culture of the organizations that use them. In one of my career roles, I purposely defied the mandate from our headquarters to "deploy" one of the packaged programs that, throughout the enterprise, was becoming quite a fad. Senior HR leaders espoused that participation in this program was "life-changing" and one of the most positive learning experiences they had ever gone through. While the learning package was polished and attractive on the surface, I found the concepts conveyed and teaching methods to be superficial and without any relevant application to the different work environments of the class participants. The designers and facilitators of the learning package had not given much thought to what might need to be put in place to reinforce some of the concepts, and the learning objectives conveyed did not have a direct relationship to the leadership standards espoused by the corporate leadership team. After several years of enforcing the "deployment" of this learning package and after spending millions of dollars, I observed that no measurable impact was realized with either individuals' behaviors or desired organizational, people-related key performance indicators.

The scenario I describe here compels all of us in mid-level operational or functional roles to carefully reflect on the ethical "balance" we strive to maintain in our careers. When should we just "shut up," keep whacking the moles, and go along with initiatives or projects that we know beyond a shadow of a doubt are doomed for failure, and when should we take a firm stance against such endeavors? Sometimes, it may be prudent to just "shut up" and decide to either make a personal change or take an alternate approach to working within the organization.

Any leader in any discipline who is determined to enhance their performance, capability, and contribution to their organization should carefully assess the following criteria for determining the quality of the learning and developmental experiences and ask the following questions:

1. Are the learning and knowledge outcomes clearly defined and measurable? Can I see the direct connection to my current or anticipated roles and responsibilities within the organization?
2. Have I been assigned to the learning experience, or have I voluntarily participated in the learning experience based on an objective assessment and observation of my behavior or knowledge?
3. Can I immediately apply the knowledge gained or the prescribed behavior to a situation where a measurable impact on an individual, team, or organizational performance can be readily observed and validated?
4. If the learning experience occurs in a formal or virtual classroom setting, am I comfortable with the learning environment? Do I feel "safe" to actively participate, learn from potential mistakes, and share the learning experience with other classroom participants?
5. Are there structures and resources available to provide direct observation, feedback, and coaching by a leader proficient in the area being developed?
6. Does the learning experience meet the organization's cultural expectations for behavior and performance, i.e., will my demonstration of the learned behavior align with the organization's expectations?

One key question we have heard through the years from leaders who have spent hundreds of hours and thousands of dollars enrolled and engaged in various leadership development experiences relates to the level of difficulty one might experience attempting to develop skills that have been identified as critical gaps for the leader. The Eichinger and Pearman framework for assessing and developing leadership "best practices" recognizes the leadership skills that are the "easiest" and the "hardest" to develop. Some of the easiest skills to develop – based on their research, are transparency, managing tasks or projects, managing information, solving problems, planning, and acquiring technical or functional skills. Some of the hardest skills to develop are leading change and transitions, navigating uncertainty and ambiguity, managing conflict, demonstrating political savvy and agility, leveraging information, demonstrating systems thinking, and, ironically, developing others! These observations imply that if certain positions or roles in the organization require some of those "hardest" to develop skills and the talent available internally does not possess those skills, then external recruiting for that talent with those skills may be necessary. We have seen numerous examples of time and money wasted trying to help someone with "square" capabilities be asked to prepare for a "round" role. In simpler terms, we should not waste time and effort trying to prepare a square peg to fit into a round mole hole! Worse yet, when organizations attempt to fit a square peg into a round hole, it infuriates the moles, and they appear with greater frequency and intensity. ***Whack, Whack, Whack!***

Finally, we offer the following set of alternative development methods, generically described in ascending order of effectiveness, to assess the quality of the learning experiences leaders engage in.

LEADERSHIP WHACK-A-MOLE

GUIDE TO ALTERNATIVE DEVELOPMENT METHODS
BY RIC SHRIVER

The following guide provides alternatives to typical classroom or formal education learning.
An effective individual development plan will incorporate some of the following methods in addition to classroom learning.

Method	Description	Outcome	Effectiveness
Reading	Reading a book, article, or other document that provides insight and knowledge about a particular topic/issue/competency.	Increased knowledge or insight – expanded awareness.	Limited in changing behavior – can expand knowledge and awareness.
Observing/ Viewing	Observe the behavior or action being performed by someone deemed as exceeding expectations in this area – it can be done live or virtually.	A visual impression, which, if viewed regularly, can positively impact the vision the learner has, can drive the creative subconscious to compel modified behavior.	Disciplined and consistent viewing can help modify a behavior or action.
Job Shadowing	Similar to the preceding method. However, this would require actually going "on-site" to observe the behavior in action from an exceeding-expectation performer.	In addition to creating a visual image of the desired behavior or action, this method enables the learner to interact with the leader, modeling the desired behavior to gain further clarification and insight.	Moderately effective depending upon the receptiveness of both the learner and leader modeling the behavior.
Mentoring	A competent leader, preferably within the	When a leader whom the learner admires	Effective, depending upon the

LEADERSHIP WHACK-A-MOLE

Method	Description	Outcome	Effectiveness
	same geographic business unit, is someone who can observe, provide honest feedback and interaction, and sound advice and coaching to the learner.	and respects outside of the formal organizational reporting hierarchy provides sound advice and coaching to enable further development	receptiveness of both the learner and the mentor.
Project/ Initiative Participation	Requires that the learner takes a role or part in a sanctioned team or group that requires the effective demonstration of the desired competency or behavior.	Both cognitive and behavior/motor skills can be developed with proper coaching and guidance from an exceeding-expectations leader.	Very effective with the right coach and mentor.
Project/ Initiative Accountability	Requires that the learner perform the competency or action individually while executing a real assignment.	Both cognitive and behavior/motor skills can be developed with proper coaching and guidance from an exceeding-expectations leader.	Very effective with the right coach and mentor; low-risk opportunities should be considered.
Job Redesign	Involves redesigning the tasks associated with the job to include tasks that require more frequent use/demonstration of the competency being developed.	Both cognitive and behavior/motor skills can be developed with proper coaching and guidance from an exceeding-expectations leader.	Most effective with the relevant responsibilities and the right coach and mentor.

LEADERSHIP WHACK-A-MOLE

THE IMPORTANCE OF HAVING A TALENT DEVELOPMENT STRATEGY

A more comprehensive and robust approach to addressing formal leadership development would be for the organization to plan, design, and implement a talent development strategy. A talent development strategy should address what we need our leaders to do today and into the future to support our business priorities. In my role as a corporate leader for Learning and Organizational Development, I was fortunate to have the backing and the confidence of our senior leadership team that our talent management strategy was critical to the success of our mission, vision, and values. The expressed desire for our talent development strategy and platform was to ***enable the organization to ensure that the right people are selected for the right reasons to perform the right duties in the right way to produce the right outcomes consistent with our organization's key performance indicators.*** The key elements of a sound talent strategy include the following:

1. A Talent Philosophy that outlines the main traits and elements of the talent development strategy with a common language to promote understanding and alignment.
2. Carefully and clearly defined roles, responsibilities, and best practices for all levels of leadership and individual contributors, consistent with the business priorities and espoused cultural values.
3. Sound selection processes to ensure that the right people are being employed for the right reasons to do the right things for the best business outcomes.

4. Ongoing talent review and validation processes to support succession planning, career development, and overall development planning for all levels of the organization.
5. Well-designed and resourced coaching and mentoring throughout the organization to ensure accountability for continuous growth and improvement.

JEFF'S RESPONSE TO RIC'S QUEST FOR LEADERSHIP EFFECTIVENESS

Identifying leadership competencies can be a challenging – and not consistently accurate – endeavor. As Ric noted, there are many programs in the marketplace that assist in identifying and developing competencies. Most of them miss the mark in terms of seeing leadership competencies as "strategic" and "adaptive." They focus primarily on *today's* competencies agreed to by job incumbents or selected from a collective survey from a vendor. That's great...*if nothing changes*. However, changes will occur, internally and externally, and the competencies needed by leaders will change. An effective leadership development program must adapt and keep current with those changes.

"Leadership" has hundreds of definitions, so why should we expect leadership development programs to have consistency across so many of them? They don't. I regularly read studies and surveys that were done to determine effective leader competencies. And the results are different from study to study. Some competencies are common in leadership studies and development programs. But this commonality depends on which of the two domains of leadership you look at. The first domain is the "traditional" roles of leaders (creating vision, planning, organization design, assuring sales and profitability, developing control mechanisms, financial management, and so on). The second domain is the "adaptive" leader role. This domain focuses on the skills needed to adapt the organization to meet changing market demands and external factors such as technology, economy, and global competition.

"Traditional" leadership development is predominant in most industries today. Change is occurring at hyper-speed in many markets, and traditional methods for developing leaders alone are insufficient for adapting to (or surviving) the changes. I find companies running leader development programs where participants read a book (while they are excellent books, are we still reading *Good to Great*? (2001) and *In Search of Excellence*? (1982)). They then attend a class discussion on the book – with perhaps a fun activity thrown in. (In my experience, many participants don't bother reading the book.) Ric emphasized that the development methods mentioned in his chart, such as job redesign and involvement in projects, are more effective because they provide an experiential, practical, relevant, and hands-on approach. However, the content offered by these methods remains "traditional" and not" adaptive."

Competencies for today's leaders have changed. We now see a greater need for strategic and systems thinking, adaptability, cross-functional team guidance, adapting to changing customer expectations, decentralized decision-making, values integration, culture adjustment, and change management. We also see power distribution, setting direction, artificial intelligence, and analyzing external information and trends needed as skills. And the faster the markets and external environments change, the greater the need for new competencies. As an example, take Covid-19. As I drive by and see the companies that have shuttered their doors, I realize they didn't have adaptive competencies in their leadership ranks. They didn't know how to adapt to a fast-changing situation, and the company died. Businesses that adapted to new ways of operating, like sit-down restaurants turning into takeout establishments or retail stores focusing on online sales, survived.

Simply presenting information in a leadership development program is not enough. The learning mode and skill application to the job are critical. Studies at the Center for Creative Leadership (CCL) (McCall et al., 1988) show that classroom training has limited effectiveness in developing successful leaders. This type of training is abundant in the marketplace but has limited effectiveness in developing successful leaders. The $166 billion estimated cost (Westfall, 2019) for leadership development shows the predominance of traditional training and development content and methods sold in the marketplace. Development candidates whose learning experiences include job rotation, mentoring, project teams, case studies, and learning from mistakes are more likely to successfully transition to leadership roles.

There are many assignments and experiences that help develop leaders. A particularly effective one is learning from mistakes – if you have a mentor or coach who can help you learn from them. Starting, managing, and leading a project – especially a cross-functional one – can also be a great development experience. Again, one needs someone to "guide" them through the learning (a higher-level manager or expert peer, for example). Practical leadership development experiences are almost always guided by a more skillful mentor or teacher, not by the Learning & Development or Human Resources departments. Sitting in a classroom or a virtual, self-paced course will not produce the skills and experiences needed to grow as a leader. One must get out of the classroom and do the things necessary to develop leadership skills.

LEADERSHIP WHACK-A-MOLE

Traditional leadership development programs miss the mark with a "one size fits all" approach. Each leader's situation is unique, including factors like the environment, culture, and management styles. Leadership development needs to be personalized and focused on developing skills through real-world experiences, not just classroom presentations. For candidates selected for promotion or succession, we will customize development plans to the business' strategic needs and challenges. With changing environments and markets, leaders at all levels will need new adaptive skills. Lower-level managers will be developed for higher-level positions, including the senior level. Decision-making will be decentralized, giving more power to middle managers, supervisors, and individual contributors to innovate new products and processes. These will be critical skills needed to adapt and flourish, and mid-level managers will be the ones to facilitate this change.

Longitudinal research at the Center for Creative Leadership (CCL) found that experiences and assignments are most important to a leader's development and success (McCall et al., 1988). Earlier, Ric mentioned the 70-20-10 model (Pedler, 1997) contributed to by Robert Eichenger at the CCL. According to this model, a leader's development is made up of 70 percent challenging experiences and assignments, 20 percent developmental relationships, and 10 percent coursework and training. This is how successful leaders learn and develop. As will be discussed in the upcoming section of talent selection, abilities (and potential for developing them) such as adaptability, agility, and strategic thinking will become foremost in the leader development process. We'll hire and promote people with these capabilities and "adaptive" skills, as well as experience and current competencies.

LESSONS LEARNED

Leadership Development - Becoming an Effective Leader

1. We need a talent development strategy to enable the organization to ensure that the right people are selected for the right reasons to perform the right duties in the right way to produce the right outcomes consistent with our organization's key performance indicators.

2. We still need to develop "traditional" competencies in leaders. We also need to focus our efforts on developing "adaptive" competencies.

3. Markets and environmental conditions are changing at lightning speed. We may face organizational demise if we don't quickly develop our next-generation leaders to adapt the business and its people to these changes.

4. Leader competencies align with the life cycle of the business. We must develop competencies specific to each stage of the cycle or we will need to replace current leaders with leaders who possess the necessary competencies.

5. Information-dispensing training is insufficient for development. We need experiential methods, coaching, and mentoring that are more effective in building competencies than classroom or virtual programs.

6. Why are we spending $166 billion (Westfall, 2019) billion a year on leadership development programs that are not developing adaptive competencies? This may be a strong indicator of what's lacking in leadership development today and the power of marketing the "traditional" programs senior leaders purchase.

Chapter 3

Sustaining Leader Motivation

Persistence in the Mole Hunt

CHALLENGE QUESTIONS FOR THE READER:

1. What role do your beliefs and values play in driving/determining your motivation as a leader?
2. Younger generations expect work to provide a meaningful sense of purpose. What do you do to help your employees find that purpose?
3. Do your personal vision and values align with those of your organization?

RIC'S SELF-EXAMINATION JOURNEY

As I reflect on the emotions I was experiencing that cold February morning in North Atlanta on my 43rd birthday, I wonder how I managed to survive over the next three decades. The future seemed depressing, overwhelming, and devoid of joy! I did survive, but I did not thrive. There were so many things I needed to do to fully enjoy life, personally and professionally. I sought help from a professional counselor who promoted "Christian Counseling," but their recommended approach was to sell everything we owned as a family and devote a couple of years to overseas missionary work. That option was not at all appealing to me or my family. I also considered looking at a less demanding role in a smaller community where the demands I was facing as an executive and the two hours of daily commute time in a city of 6 million people might have helped me get a grip on my work-life balance. But leaving Atlanta was not an attractive option for my family at the time – they had friends and family there and, to this day, have remained there. So, for the next two decades, I attempted to maneuver the professional and personal challenges that life presented without truly understanding how to fully maximize the impact I desired to have on the important relationships in my life and my career.

The path that I perceived to be the "responsible" path was to continue giving my career all that I could to responsibly support my family. To do that required more travel, relocation, broader responsibilities, and the surrender to a lifestyle and lifestyle habits that ultimately damaged my physical, mental, emotional, and spiritual health. Ultimately, I sacrificed my family and my financial well-being, both of which forced me to finally, after another two decades, take a hard look at the direction my life had gone, the pain that I had experienced and had caused to so many along the way, and what genuinely aligned with my foundational values, passions, and goals.

I remember the evening, once again on my birthday in February, when I made the decision to voluntarily step into a less demanding role within the company - a role consistent with my natural interests and passions. Fortunately, I worked for two managing executives who fully supported my decision and provided continued support as I worked through the transition over the next few months. I continue to be thankful for their support! The decision to make the change was costly financially, but what I have gained since refocusing my life far outweighs the money I left behind.

LEADERSHIP WHACK-A-MOLE

There are some key lessons I can confidently convey to the reader who may be struggling with challenges like the ones I have outlined above:

1. Know, confirm, and regularly reinforce your personal values and beliefs – do not let work, other people, careers, or outside activities compel you to sacrifice those values!
2. Know your personal preferences, passions, and natural talents. There are numerous tools and assessments to help us recognize where our true career passions lie. Once known, seek opportunities professionally that support and enable the full deployment of those passions, preferences, and talents. As a good friend and mentor, Bob Moawad, told me in a personal communication years ago, "Do what you love to do, do it as well as you can, and you'll never have to work another day in your life!"
3. Carefully assess your current environment and honestly ask yourself, "Are there expectations, behaviors, or practices that contradict, or worse, compel me to sacrifice my personal values to "fit in"? If the answer to this question is "yes," make plans to find another place to contribute. Toxic corporate environments, like toxic people, can destroy your character and your life if left unchecked.
4. Consistent with the above assessment, carefully assess the cultures you may consider for potential employment. Ask yourself if the actual values of the organization align with your values, and are the organization's decisions, actions, and outcomes reflecting what their values espouse?

We often ask ourselves, "What am I truly motivated to do?" As leaders, we also struggle to understand what "motivates" the members of our teams. While there are many motivational models, one I have always found helpful is Victor Vroom's Expectancy Model (1964). Simply stated, Vroom's model is based on 1) a belief and level of confidence (or expectancy) that we can successfully accomplish whatever it is we are considering doing and 2) trust that if we carry out the action, both desired intrinsic and extrinsic rewards will be achieved. The key factor influencing the level of motivation we need to start the task is the degree of confidence - or comfort - we have in our ability to perform it successfully. Reflecting on my career experiences, the confidence factor underscores the importance and value of the coaching and support we receive. A healthy, well-aligned organization will create an environment where a leader's confidence and attitude are reinforced and supported, providing comfort, confidence, and peace. This was observed in a leadership team gathering by a career-long colleague and friend of mine, Suzanne Hoonan:

"I was a recent guest invited to participate with a group of corporate decision-makers. It was a fascinating experience and one I have thought about at length. I wondered why I left that lengthy meeting feeling so hopeful and confident.

"The group was comprised of influential leaders who exhibited behaviors that resulted in those feelings. How did they do that?

"I have identified several things I witnessed that go to those powerful Increasing Human Effectiveness concepts again. If I was FEELING hopeful and confident, then WORDS and PICTURES were surely responsible. I saw a group of collaborative, professional, goal-oriented people working together toward the common good and toward success, always toward success. Their WORDS triggered PICTURES, which resulted in FEELINGS, which is the thought process we have all

been taught. Egos were set aside. Respect prevailed. No one needed the spotlight. There was no disparaging of ideas. There were differences and debates, but there was a lack of judgment regarding positions on topics. Body language was engaged, attentive, and friendly. I did not see one eye roll, shaking head, scowl, or otherwise negative message. The entire meeting continued in this happy, collaborative vibe! It was special. Humor was present and was enjoyed by all. Sarcasm was not the tone, but rather, it was light-hearted and silly banter that was consistent.

"We know that a collaborative culture is based on openness, just like a lifesaving parachute. That requires transparency and trust. Energies must be used to search for solutions to challenges and leverage opportunities. No blame, no searching for guilt. Look internally as well as externally.

"Leadership sets the tone – always has, always will. Passion, commitment, respect, and follow-through must be employed. Our workforce will know if these qualities are present or not. I could tell that these leaders communicated often and with purpose. They were methodical in their approach to what was communicated and how. In the end, we know that our culture and the way we interact and engage is the single most important thing we can build and maintain. Focus on it every day!" (Hoonan & Associates, 2023, used with permission)

Suzanne's account tells us a great deal about the motivating potential of workplace culture and leadership behavior.

In the leadership classes that I have facilitated, I begin the classes by asking the participants what their primary expectations are for the class. Nearly every group I pose that question to says, "I want to learn how to motivate my team!" If I had exposed my true thoughts, my instinctive response to that question would have been to tell the participants right up front that they alone cannot motivate the people they lead. But I did, without fail, restrain my instinctive response. At some point during my time together with the group, I stressed the importance of creating the kind of culture and environment where people will be motivated to do the right things for the right reasons to achieve the right outcomes for the team, customers, and clients they serve. The desire and will to create a successful team environment as leaders require us to align with our company's values and fully utilize our individual strengths and passions. We hope that these conditions exist within the minds of our senior leaders. If these conditions are met, the kind of observations Suzanne Hoonan describes above will become a reality.

Suzanne references a personal development class that I have had the opportunity to facilitate throughout most of my career – *Increasing Human Effectiveness* (2021). Bob Mowad, founder of Edge Learning, created the class curriculum. The fundamental principles conveyed and reinforced throughout the class show the power that we all have as leaders. Our intent should be to create a culture and environment where team members can "be motivated" to perform at their full potential and produce positive outcomes. Hiring the right people with values consistent with the organization's is one of the most important actions we must execute as leaders. The next chapter will elaborate on the "selection" process and the significant impact it has on managing performance.

LEADERSHIP WHACK-A-MOLE

JEFF'S RESPONSE TO RIC'S SELF-EXAMINATION JOURNEY

Ric captures the journey and situation many of us have gone through in our careers – staying motivated and engaged by aligning our values with those of the company and team. We then feel that we are living, reinforcing, and working on our values. I want to know that my values are as important to my employer and manager as they are to me. We understand how difficult it can be to work in an organization where our values don't align.

As a consultant, I was told a story about an employee who had a strong value alignment with an organization they worked in for many years. The company values were focused on both the customers and the employees. There was a strong sense of teamwork throughout the company and in their department. When their manager left the company, their bosses brought in a new leader whose values were different. The new manager was very detached from the team. Their behavior broke the team into two adversarial teams. The manager's strong value not to "expose our dirty laundry" within or outside the department became evident when the employee "exposed" an internal team problem to other project members (who needed to know about the problem in order to meet their customer's expectations). The manager got quite upset and badgered the employee for two days to apologize to the offending teammate. After an unproductive meeting with the offender, the employee finally succumbed to the manager's pressure and apologized. As I was told, the offender then got up and walked out of the meeting, saying, "Well, that's a good first step." And guess what? There were no other steps. That was it! Nothing was ever said or done after that. The real problems were never addressed. ***Whack!***

LEADERSHIP WHACK-A-MOLE

In the preceding story and after the value "violation," trust was broken, and communication stopped. Team harmony vanished. Apparently, next-level management was informed about the situation and took no action – not even to investigate what happened. Silence reigned! After two years of trying to stay true to their values under a new manager who endorsed different values, the employee's original value alignment was damaged. It was time for them to move on. Their positive attitude took a hit! ***Whack!*** Quite sad for this person after working for such a strong, values-based company for so many years. This speaks to the dissolution of culture. In a strong culture, new hires are selected and onboarded and learn the company's values. Leadership is expected to model and reinforce the company values. That didn't happen in this case. It exemplifies how one leader can destroy a productive and healthy culture.

With the growth of the talent marketplace, leaders will be "hiring" a diverse population of contractors, contingent workers, and workers from other countries with different cultures and values. Adding these "others" to the workforce inserts another dimension into the value alignment dynamic. Domestically, we have great diversity in the workforce, bringing a wide range of values and beliefs. The current Diversity, Equity, and Inclusion (DEI) efforts will further emphasize an expanding array of beliefs and values. The solution is not to force people to agree with the company's values but to align them with their personal values. The workers can then experience an integration of both sets of values.

As a management consultant, I conducted workshops in values alignment where participants would identify their key personal values and align them with their organization's. There were often disconnects between the participants and the organization's values. The teams worked hard to reconcile this misalignment through spirited discussion. It led to questioning by participants about just how "real" the organization's stated values were. We often see the company's values on a poster hanging on the wall, but employees don't always believe what they see. Management must model and reinforce the values ("walk the talk"). Sometimes, in the workshops, management agreed to discuss the values with the staff. At other times, management expected staff to adhere to the professed values of the company (the ones hanging on the wall). Sometimes, staff and management agree to revise the values collaboratively.

A client of mine considered themself a "values-based" leader. They wrote the company's vision, mission, and values on a large sheet of paper, posted it in the break room, and asked all employees to sign the sheet, showing their commitment to the words on the paper. After a week, there were only a few signatures on the sheet – all senior managers. What happened here? A disconnect between what was said and how management behaved? Most likely. ***Whack!***

Numerous factors influence motivation and engagement. Vroom's Expectancy Model (that Ric discussed earlier) explains some factors: the expectation that I can achieve the task and the "reward" and whether I value it. In his book *Drive* (2009), Daniel Pink identifies "autonomy, mastery, and purpose" as key motivators. He suggests that money is not as strong a motivator for "knowledge" workers if it meets their "equity" expectations. All three of Pink's motivators are essential values for me. When I've taken internal positions, I am "driven" when these motivators are a part of the job and supported by management. While still important, compensation became a secondary issue for me. I'm willing to take a lower salary if the three motivators are there. As a management consultant, all three motivators inspired me to achieve high levels of performance.

I regularly assessed my motivation for my work to assure myself that I had a strong sense of "drive."

A commonly accepted belief in the world of work is that human motivation is both internal and external to the person. While this is true, internal motivation is typically stronger than external (particularly, as Pink identified for non-routine work). Values are a component of internal motivators and can be quite powerful in their effect.

During college, I worked in an airplane parts factory that made components for jet planes. My job was to run a manual eight-bit drill press to bore symmetrical holes in aluminum adapter rings for the aircraft engines. It was the most boring job I've ever had, spending eight hours a day navigating the drill press up and down, up and down, up and down. After the holes were drilled, I scoped each with a gauge. I threw those rings that met the specifications into a bin marked "accepted;" those not meeting the specifications went into the "unacceptable" bin.

Many factors could have demotivated me: low pay, a tedious job, standing for eight hours (no breaks, only a 30-minute lunch), a hot, non-air-conditioned factory, extreme noise from all the production machines, no one to talk to, four-hour bus rides each day, and a supervisor who only spoke to me when I made an error. My *values* and *purpose* kept me going. The adapter rings I was drilling were to be installed in jet planes. Every time I ran that press, I thought about how my performance and outcomes could have killed pilots, crew, and passengers. One mistake – not caught -could endanger the life of any one of them. I tell this story to exemplify the strength of internal motivators despite strong external demotivators. Without a strong purpose, I'd have been ripe for a union organizer.

Let's talk more about ***purpose***. We see purpose as a prerequisite for many workers in the Millennial (1981-96) and Generation Z (1997-2012), and soon in Generation Alpha (2010-25) cohorts. Purpose has played a role in all generations (think of The Greatest Generation (1901-27) during World War II). The "problem" today is that younger-generation workers are looking for their purpose in work – ***not necessarily*** the business' purpose. When discussing this with leaders, the most common response I hear is that the purpose of the business is to "make money." It's sad when workers have a sense of purpose for their work, and that purpose doesn't align with the business'. Like value alignment, purpose misalignment can lead to demotivated workers and attrition in the workforce.

Leaders must consider a worker's purpose, as it instills motivation and meaning in one's work. As I described in my story about working at the airplane parts factory, an individual can be motivated intrinsically through their sense of purpose. Working with non-profits and charities, I saw members having a strong sense of purpose in their work (through the execution of the mission). In my experience, their motivation, productivity, engagement, and job satisfaction were often greater than those of workers in the private and government sectors. Leaders - especially managers - must help workers see the connection between their purpose and the organization's. "Purpose" should be a part of routine conversations between managers and their employees.

Work cultures are changing. Environmental, market, and workforce conditions force organizations to rethink motivation and engagement. We have already addressed some internal motivators:

autonomy, mastery, and purpose. We continue to see turbulent changes in the external environment (the economy, pandemics, global competition) that can affect motivation. The old Industrial Age forms of motivation don't work well today. Markets are changing. Consumers are more informed and demanding than they were previously. Supply chains are now global. Today's employees want to work with purpose. Self-managed, cross-functional teams will be necessary, and so will the motivators that drive them. It is time to reevaluate how we design the work, the work environment, and the management practices that inspire our teams to motivate themselves to higher levels of performance and quality outcomes.

LESSONS LEARNED
Sustaining Leader Motivation

1. Beliefs and values are an essential part of leadership (and all) motivation.
2. In its simplest terms, motivation is strongest when we believe we can accomplish the task and the reward will be achieved and valued (Expectancy Theory).
3. Personal and organizational vision and values must align for the greatest motivation.
4. Daniel Pink (2009) identified "autonomy, mastery, and purpose" as key motivators.
5. Younger generations expect to have a sense of purpose in their work and their organizations.

✱✱✱

Chapter 4

Managing Performance

Maximizing Performance in Spite of The Moles

CHALLENGE QUESTIONS FOR THE READER:

1. Does your current Performance Management system support your organization's changing strategies and culture?

2. Do your job descriptions include the skills and abilities of the candidate needed for future employee deployment to teams and positions?

3. Is your training performance-based and applied to the job, or is it informational "downloads?"

4. What are the deficiencies in your performance appraisal process? How do employees and leaders feel about performance appraisal? Is the system fair and equitable?

5. When someone is not performing as expected, do you look at possible causes besides the individual?

Performance Management is the combination of structure and processes that ensure that job responsibilities are defined, qualified candidates are sourced, hired, on boarded, trained to perform the job as defined, developed to gain new skills, prepared for career advancement, and that the performer is expected to self-evaluate – and if necessary, correct - overall performance.

LEADERSHIP WHACK-A-MOLE

RIC ADDRESSES THE PERFORMANCE MANAGEMENT CHALLENGE

Most of us who have assumed leadership responsibilities aspire to make a positive difference in whatever environment we find ourselves in. We expect the same of the people we are responsible for. However, we are often perplexed throughout our careers by "what constitutes a positive difference?" In my first leadership role in the non-profit organization, which I referenced in Chapter 1, there were five measures against which my performance and the performance of my direct reports were assessed: 1) Attitude, 2) Punctuality, 3) Quality, 4) Communication, and 5) Ethical Compliance. The company had a one-page document to evaluate these five "attributes," and as managers, we used a 5-point Likert scale (1932) to "measure" the perceived effectiveness of our direct reports in each area. There was no "self-evaluation" – only a manager's subjective assessment of a direct report's performance in these five areas. As I recall my early "evaluations," in all but one of the categories assessed, I excelled with "5" ratings. The one category I received a "4" on was quality. Much of my job at the time involved carefully analyzing compensation, payroll, benefits, and cost information. Early in my career, I found that "attention to detail" was not my forte (particularly when the other seven members of the Personnel Department were creating constant distractions)!

So, as leaders, we ask ourselves, "What constitutes strong performance, and how can we effectively measure and improve upon it in our roles?" To establish a firm foundation and framework for effective performance management, I have found that there are a number of key questions leaders and their organizations should ask themselves:

LEADERSHIP WHACK-A-MOLE

1. Do you have a clear understanding of and reinforcement for your organization and department/unit's purpose/mission? Is that purpose shared and regularly reinforced?

2. Do you clearly define goals and desired outcomes at the organizational, department/unit, and personal levels?

3. Do you have a clear and regularly updated understanding of your primary customers' needs, and are you regularly aligning your personal and department/unit priorities with those needs?

4. Are you regularly examining, evaluating, and assessing the effectiveness of the core processes within your area of responsibility to ensure that they are focused on the primary internal and external customer needs?

5. Are you regularly examining, evaluating, and assessing the roles and responsibilities of the people supporting core processes to ensure that you have the right people doing the right things in the right way to ensure the best outcomes?

6. Given the scope of your services, do you feel that you are adequately resourced with the correct number and kinds of people, materials, equipment, information, and time to serve your primary customers' needs effectively?

7. Are you regularly and consistently providing feedback and communication regarding the effectiveness and impact of your area(s) of responsibility on the primary customers you serve…and the entire organization?

8. Are you and your team examining, evaluating, and assessing to what degree your department/unit complies with the regulatory standards governing your department/unit?

JEFF EXPOUNDS ON PERFORMANCE MANAGEMENT TRENDS

Ric's description of his organization's performance evaluation tool and process gives us insight into the subjectivity of traditional performance management. A positive for Ric was that he learned that attention to detail was not his strength. Many workers possess strengths that are not used in their "jobs," and not utilizing them is a loss for the business. By knowing his strengths and weaknesses, he could redeploy his Human Resources career in a direction that utilized his strengths.

Although the nature and structure of work are changing, the performance management process remains the same. What needs to change is to focus on the new skills, tasks, traits, and requirements for work. Organizational structures will change with more emphasis on cross-functional communities, multi-level communication, artificial intelligence, remote and hybrid work, generational differences, and project or ad-hoc teams. Today, we give "timed" performance feedback – annually or quarterly. In adaptive organizations, managers and teams will provide instantaneous feedback on an ongoing basis. Individual development planning will be individualized for employees and managers with the most significant potential and those with the right skills (and the capabilities to learn new skills) for promotion or redeployment to new positions or projects.

LEADERSHIP WHACK-A-MOLE

Great changes are coming! Our Industrial Age performance management practices will someday catch up with the demands of the current Digital Age. Too many highly qualified employees are quitting their companies because of a lack of career and skill development opportunities. Progressive companies will require a "talent marketplace," where new, current, and future jobs will be filled by a range of candidates – incumbents, part-time, contract, off-shore, freelancers, and "gig" workers to provide a broader selection pool and faster candidate deployment into jobs or projects. Individual goals will be flexible, changeable, and tied closely to the company's core business and strategic objectives (which will likely change before the annual performance review). Jobs will no longer use only market value and job requirements for compensation, but of increasingly greater importance will be "pay for skills, experience, and capabilities" as companies look for unique and vital skills to help them today and into the future. Compensation will be perceived as "inequitable" for some workers with fewer necessary "strategic" skills. The path to higher compensation, then, will be based on developing skills that the company deems critical to the enterprise's current and future performance, as well as on job performance and results.

As the nature of jobs changes, so will the manager's role. Unlike today's role of "controller" of tasks and projects, we already see the importance of the coaching and mentoring role. As organizations become more trans-functional and team-focused, managers will be more critical in guiding individuals to be effective "team players" and skill builders for redeployed roles. This will change the character of performance management as human capital forecasting, recruitment, selection, training, coaching, compensation, and appraisal adapt to the "new work organization."

Performance management will explode with the expansion of Artificial Intelligence (AI). While 85 million jobs will likely be eliminated with AI, 97 million jobs will be created. (Iacoviello, 2023) AI will eliminate some jobs, but many jobs will be integrated with AI. Workers will need to learn to work with AI tools throughout their careers. AI will be involved in every dimension of performance management. It's coming fast, and we need to prepare for it now.

Performance management today continues to be a relic of the Industrial Age job structure and organizational design. The lengthy hiring processes that we have today (waiting months to hear back about the hiring decision and far too many interviews) will need to become faster, agile processes to capture the "qualified" candidates in a shorter period. We will emphasize hiring agile learners who can develop into generalists with broad skills. We can also assess the skills range of incumbent workers and reskill to meet the demands of the business. Most jobs will soon require new skills. We need to prepare for this in how we manage performance. All this begins with the first of the five performance management components discussed in this chapter - a job and skill definition tied to the changing business' current and future "strategic" needs.

THE REALM OF PERFORMANCE MANAGEMENT

Traditionally, performance management encompasses all aspects of managing the performance of individuals and teams, including:

1. Defining the job.
2. Selecting the right "talent" for the job.
3. Developing and coaching the talent.

4. Creating a successful and impactful performance review process.
5. Understanding and dealing with performance problems.

In this chapter, we will break down the performance management process within the framework of these five performance management components.

1. Defining the Job – *Determining How We Work Amidst the Moles*

JEFF TALKS ABOUT DEFINING JOBS AND WORK EXPECTATIONS

Historically, performance management focused on the performance of the individual worker. However, with work structures changing, middle managers are now expected to manage or coach cross-functional performance. The future trend is more self-management for individuals and teams, where self-evaluation and team assessments of an individual's performance will support the manager's evaluation. This poses the question of the manager's future role.

How does one define a job? Traditionally, those familiar with the purpose and functions needed for the position create the job description. A job description is usually written to cover the job's purpose, functions, and requirements. The job description is a quasi-legal document used in performance appraisal and corrective or other employment actions. The document is highly structured and typically includes an overview of the job, the job functions (especially the "essential" ones), necessary competencies, training or education, and other relevant elements. An often-used phrase in job descriptions is "other duties as assigned," which, in my experience, means anything else the manager decides to give you (relevant to the job or not). The job description requirements become the foundation for selecting, managing, and evaluating staff.

The above explanation of how a job description is designed sounds logical and reasonable. Analyze the job, write a description, and utilize the product. However, wait! There's more! Job descriptions are often tied to compensation. One way to value a job is to assess the job's requirements in terms of market conditions. A doctor's "value" to the organization is evaluated as "greater" than a lab tech in a hospital setting. Hence, the doctor's compensation is higher than the lab tech's based on job requirements, required education and certification/licensing, organizational needs, and market conditions.

Larger businesses typically use a structured template to design the job description, which tends to be more accurate than the hundreds of "homemade" descriptions I've seen from smaller companies, assuming they have them at all. Job descriptions serve a function – they tell the performer the "big picture" and the tasks required of the job. Given the legal challenges over the past several decades, job descriptions are documents that can protect an employer and/or employee from potential legal liability. Rigid job descriptions are a relic of Industrial Age thinking, even though they continue to have widespread application today.

Jobs today are changing. They are becoming more team-focused, more autonomous, requiring more innovation, and becoming more networked across the organization. This makes it difficult for managers to "stick to the script" of managing an individual's or team's performance from a defined and static job description. Individual contributors and teams will make decisions independent of managers but still need to be overseen by the manager. Teams will select (and remove) their team members – not just managers. Just one manager cannot manage networked teams – the team must self-manage. How will a manager "appraise" the performance of a cross-company project team? When teams start appraising themselves and their members, how will a traditional job description help?

Perhaps job descriptions should have skill requirements (as appropriate to the position) but also include skills more relevant to the changing nature of jobs: critical thinking, evaluating, and aligning personal vision and values with the organization's, innovation, agility, leading self-managed teams, autonomy, self-development, impact on customer (external or internal) satisfaction, emotional intelligence, and so on. More organizations today are moving away from selecting based primarily on education and training and more on agility and adaptability. Some organizations have evolved to an outcome- or skills-based job definition.

We must find other, more adaptable ways to define jobs, including the changes cited in the preceding paragraph. Changes are coming faster and faster, and past performance management methods must adapt. We can still define jobs, but those definitions must be flexible and more open to the continually changing nature of jobs and organizational strategies. Moreover, we'll need to figure out how to "legalize" the changes in managing performance. The survival of many businesses is at stake if we don't change soon. Moreover, making job descriptions more flexible – and outcome- and skill-based - can be a first step in that direction.

RIC'S RESPONSE TO DEFINING JOBS AND WORK EXPECTATIONS

Jeff's assessment of the need for more flexibility and adaptability in designing and administering job descriptions is spot on! Job descriptions should be living, breathing "digital documents" that can be modified as work, service, and product delivery processes are altered and updated by the ongoing monitoring and gathering of market intelligence. However, the question is, who does the updating? Moreover, if the job description continues to be the basis for determining the scope, specifications, physical and mental requirements, and overall intent for the role, who and how should the ongoing maintenance and communication of the documents be managed? I agree with Jeff regarding the role of the entire team, department, or process unit in continuously reviewing the essential duties and requirements for the various roles that support the processes serving internal and external clients and customers. While we collectively want to ensure that the essential duties and scope of the jobs/roles in question are important, the real focus should be on the evolution of knowledge, skills, and abilities (competencies) required to perform the essential duties now and, most importantly, *into the future*. So, when it comes to formal appraisals, I strongly support and recommend a primary focus on individual and team development with a continued focus on the customer/client's expectations for quality and value.

As we think about clearly documenting roles, responsibilities, and expected behavioral competencies within a functional team, the question of "accountability" arises – "Who is responsible for what, under what circumstances, and for what ultimate purpose or outcome?" I can humorously recall playing Little League baseball when I was a child. As I was learning to play baseball at the age of 7 or 8, the coach of my team would typically assign me to either the right field…or wherever the opposing team usually did not hit the ball! I struggled. However, I did improve and ultimately moved to the center field position. One of the biggest challenges I faced playing the center field position was determining who, in the outfield positions, should "have the ball" when it was hit outside the infield. The team coach was emphatic about one of us shouting out,

"I've got it," when we were confident the ball was in our respective "zones." The accountability for catching and returning the ball to the appropriate infield player was built into our "essential duties" defined by the coach. When one of us made the "I've got it" call, we had to be confident that we could properly field the ball without error. I have found that with many of the functional teams I have been affiliated with and/or overseen, there is sometimes a reluctance to shout out (figuratively), "I've got it!" In organizational cultures with lower levels of engagement, few people often desire to take responsibility – or "ownership" – for the work that needs to be done

I spent most of my career in Human Resources (HR) related leadership roles. My experiences in several different organizations confirmed my beliefs that it is sometimes challenging to clarify and reinforce the assigned roles within the department. Once clarified and confirmed, job descriptions should clearly document what each member of the department is responsible for. I suspect that the challenges outlined below are present in many business functions – HR is not alone!

Leaders in most organizations know that the "HR" Department has five primary Performance Management responsibilities – 1) Recruit qualified candidates for open positions; 2) Screen and support the selection of viable candidates for open positions; 3) Ensure a proper onboarding process is consistently and accurately completed for selected candidates; 4) Provide both a process and structure for the orientation of new employees; and 5) Work with the leaders of the organization to ensure that the tools and resources necessary to help the employees perform at their best are readily available. Believe it or not, there is often disagreement among the responsibilities described above…even among HR professionals! Recruiters often do not understand or accept the responsibility for ensuring that information critical to the onboarding process is secured from the candidate before "handing" a finalist off to the onboarding person. The onboarding person may not understand or accept the responsibility for ensuring that, once cleared for employment, new employees are consistently and accurately informed and directed to the place and time for the orientation process. Finally, once new employees have completed the orientation process, the individuals conducting and overseeing it may not understand or accept the responsibility for ensuring that the new employees are informed about where and when they will begin their official duties within the organization. There exists much potential for quite a bit of "***whacking!***"

With the significant increase of projects in the workplace and the growth of cross-functional, skill-based project teams, it is important to include the need for flexibility as a requirement in the essential functions in our job descriptions. As organizations continue to initiate new projects in response to the rapidly changing market and environment, the skills and associated work expectations needed to support those new projects will also change. This new reality requires that all members of the participating project team possess the ability to anticipate, plan for, and precisely "***whack***" the unplanned-for moles (i.e., problems) when they raise their unwelcome heads. In essence, a level of discipline to maintain both awareness and focus becomes a structural necessity in support of success.

I believe that many leaders find it difficult to understand how planned actions and defined tasks truly affect desired business outcomes. I am frequently astonished by the number of leaders I encounter who are unaware of the necessary time and resources for executing actions and tasks outlined in the job description or project plan. Ensuring that the jobs or projects we have created drive organizational results requires that, as leaders, we fully understand the amount of human effort and other resources necessary to affect the expected outcomes for the business. If this is not done accurately, then there is a high probability that unnecessary labor costs will be incurred, resulting in a loss of profitability for the enterprise. It requires that we manage our own time well and ensure that the actions and tasks delegated to the various contributors on our teams are performed in the most efficient and effective ways possible. With exempt professional and managerial talent responsibilities, we should be focused on the contribution that is being made to support our enterprise mission, goals, and objectives. Furthermore, we should have clearly defined and objective ways of measuring that impact. For non-exempt, hourly staff, a clear understanding of the time and human capabilities required to complete assigned tasks and the potential workload fluctuations that might occur is necessary. As leaders, we should possess a clear understanding and appreciation for the nature of the work being performed as we delegate those activities and tasks to the members of our teams. In previous executive-level human resources roles that I have held, I witnessed far too many resources being dedicated to actions and tasks with inadequately defined outcomes, poorly defined requirements for the talent and other resources needed to achieve the intended outcomes, and inaccurate or poorly defined ways of measuring the effectiveness of the planned actions and tasks. In short, I believe that there is much waste occurring in many types of businesses throughout the industrialized world and that, as leaders, we should be expected to be good stewards of the resources we are given to achieve the best results for the various stakeholders of our organizations. But I have also observed capable members of an organization's teams being taxed with more responsibility for positive impact and/or production than what would be considered reasonable – a perfect prescription for frustration, burnout, and eventually the loss of qualified, high potential talent.

The dilemmas outlined in the preceding paragraphs regarding the roles, responsibilities, and best practice actions or behaviors underscore the need to ensure that, as leaders and as an organization, we are placing the right people in the right jobs to ensure the right outcomes for all the stakeholders of the organization. Recruiting and selecting the right talent becomes a critical component of performance management!

2. Selecting the Right Talent - *Finding the Talent to Whack More Moles*

JEFF'S TAKE ON SELECTING TALENT

Has talent selection become an American "science?" We have studied it to death. However, we still have difficulty selecting the right people for the job. We have tests for every aspect of recruiting and selection - personality, behavior, achievement, aptitude, etc. We have decision-making templates to rank and select candidates, reference checks (which seldom garner us much information for predicting successful performance), results-based resumes, keyword resume searches, handwriting analysis (which Ric passed in a hiring process – even though his teacher scolded him in the third grade for holding his pencil the wrong way), and, of course, the illustrious conversational interview (including the behavioral version). If I sound cynical, here's why:

LEADERSHIP WHACK-A-MOLE

I taught interviewing and selection courses to local HR managers in Hong Kong. One might suspect that a cultural difference exists in the practice of Human Resources. Even though Hong Kong is a very Westernized country (although a part of China now), the culture has much Chinese influence. One HR manager took issue with my assertion that American personnel selection was "science-based" and questioned its effectiveness. While I didn't have data to substantiate my claim, I did ask her if she knew a better way. Yes, she said. She did.

This HR manager (we'll call her Victoria) worked for a traditional Chinese shipping company. She described the selection process as follows:

1. The candidate must be referred to the company's owner by a mutual connection (family in particular).
2. The company owner interviews the candidate, looking especially for signs of "character."
3. If the owner is pleased with the candidate, a battery of assessment tests is initiated.
4. The assessment "tests" included palm reading, tea leaf reading, and other prophetic tests.
5. If the candidate "passed" the tests, they would be highly considered for a position.

Victoria told me that the selection process was very effective. Most applicants who passed these steps were hired and remained on the job for many years (of course, culture played a large part in this). I couldn't argue with her testimonial of success. It made me realize that not only is talent selection affected by culture (national or organizational), but our highly science-based methodologies may be no more effective than traditional Chinese methods that Westerners might consider "fortune telling."

So, given our current state of talent selection, how do we proceed to make our selections most effective? When I taught this topic to HR graduate students at the university, I first asked the class to tell me what they believed was the most effective selection method. Almost everyone agreed that interviewing was. When I asked them for their reasoning, they told me that interviewing allowed one to "really get to know the person"- things that can't be found on a resume. That's the old, "my gut tells me that he (or she) is the one." **Whack!** However, we know that conversational interviews have limited effectiveness as a predictor of job fit and future successful performance and are filled with biases and validity and reliability limitations. The range of effectiveness of the methods can be seen in Exhibit 4.1.

The rule of thumb in selecting an applicant is this:

Use methods that are closest to actual job tasks and situations

We know the problems with reference checks. Former employers don't want to put themselves in a libelous position of reporting anything that might come back to haunt them (or sue them), so they say little or nothing about the applicant.

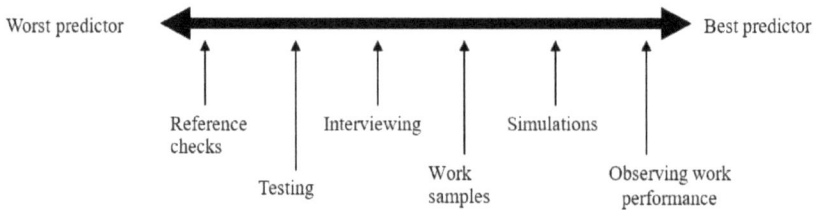

Exhibit 4.1. Continuum of selection methods and their effectiveness in predicting performance

While general testing validity has improved over time, some tests are still not good predictors of future performance. Interviewing, as we know, has several flaws, including "like me" bias, "like my uncle Bob" (who I don't like) bias, racial, religious, and gender etc. biases, lack of standardization in questioning, and more. "Behavioral" interviewing may be a somewhat better predictor of performance. As "they" say, past performance is the best predictor of future performance, but even if the context and culture differ? While I have never been trained as nor practiced as a neurosurgeon, I believe that I can "beat" a behavioral interview for such a position by painstakingly studying medical texts, especially case studies ("Tell me about a time that you botched a pre-frontal lobotomy…what did you do…what were the results?"). **Whack.** A problem today with behavioral interviewing is that responses state what happened in the past. However, the conditions, changing skills, and adaptability for the *future* are not assessed.

Work samples are a better predictor of performance but not necessarily of cultural or team fit. We assume that a candidate's work samples are original, which can be a faulty assumption (not to be cynical, but someone else may have created them). Work simulations are a better predictor of performance. For example, *assessment centers* show us how a candidate acts or decides in various situations. Regarding simulations, my brother interviewed for a sales position. A part of the interview was for him to "sell" a book of matches to the interviewer. While it might say something about my brother's sales process (in selling a book of matches) or style, it has no context in real life since my brother would be selling radio advertising to a much different demographic than the interviewer (he didn't get the job – *whack!* They didn't even let him keep the matches).

Observing work performance (especially over time) is more likely to predict successful performance because it is the actual work we observe. The downside of observing work performance is that it is difficult to watch it for any length of time to ensure the reliability of the results. Someone can perform well in a particular job or task in a specific context (for example, selling matchbooks) and culture but not in others. Finally, (although not in Exhibit 1) is the resume. Candidates have learned how to build a resume that focuses on quantified accomplishments, which gives some credence to the candidate's qualifications. However, we know from experts that a great many resumes have falsifications. Furthermore, the applicants learn the keywords for the computer scan.

Today's big issue in hiring is the "chicken and egg" debate about whether to hire for skills or cultural fit. Both are important. We can upskill a new hire to gain the capability to perform the job (unless it is dunking a basketball, which requires as much capacity as skill). While "value fit" is also important, people can shift values and beliefs if they choose to, in the proper environment and with training or guidance. The values of the business can change as well.

LEADERSHIP WHACK-A-MOLE

A new strategy regarding customer satisfaction may require a pivot in values for many staff. A case in point: My computer modem quit working the other day. I was shaking in my boots to call *THAT* communication company to fix it. After 30 years of customer "no-service" from them, I dreaded spending hours on the phone with a technician trying to get it to work. However, my interactions with the technicians on the phone were excellent. They were pleasant, helpful, and had a great attitude about trying to fix my problem. They sent a technician to my house the very same day. In the past, I had to wait for days – even weeks – for a tech to make a house call. I was elated with the service. So how, after more than 30 years as a captive customer, did a stodgy, Industrial-Age business change radically into a good customer service model? They likely didn't replace thousands of their often rude and inefficient workers in several years (the last time I received the poor service). Things were put in place (likely strategy, roles, training, reinforcers of behavior, compensation, vision, improved selection of new hires, etc.) that helped employees alter their values, beliefs, behaviors, and performance. This is a large company, so yes, it can be done.

Would I instead hire one over the other – skills or values? No, I'd look hard for the candidates who mostly have the values and skills I need for this position. There are tests for cultural fit that can predict successful alignment, but this assumes that the culture of the business will never change. Looking at today's environments and markets, this is an absurd assumption. Things are changing faster and faster, and companies must adapt their cultures to keep up with the changes. They need "right fit" candidates who can change with it.

We may wish to look at (and train for) capabilities forthcoming in the workplace: adaptability, aligning with vision, initiating and navigating changes, working in leaderless, multifunctional teams, working in lean environments, thinking critically about the business, using power constructively, and so on. We may want to start recruiting candidates with those capabilities (or who can learn them) if we wish to move employee selection positively into the turbulent future.

Selection will also become a means of finding candidates with potential for future promotional positions or roles. Examples of such potential roles include but are not limited to working in a cross-functional or networked team, accepting feedback from multiple teams that one may work on, working in a hybrid work situation, the ability to lead teams and projects, and emotional intelligence. We are no longer looking for just position qualifications in the current job description. We're hiring for the future as well – the future of the individual and the enterprise.

Generational differences in many aspects of performance management are already impacting the selection of workers. This includes flexible schedules, remote/virtual workplaces, work-life balance, competitive rewards, and increased control over their work. In my experience, many younger and entry-level workers expect to be developed and promoted quickly. When not afforded the opportunity, they leave and go to an organization that does. With the post-COVID pandemic, more workers have quit jobs (50.6 million in 2022, according to the U.S. Bureau of Labor Statistics, 2024). Companies are looking intensely for workers (incredibly hard-to-find, qualified talent). Leaders must be hyperaware of the needs of all employees, especially the Millennial and Gen-Z generations (and others to come).

LEADERSHIP WHACK-A-MOLE

There are many factors to be considered by American businesses when sourcing and selecting candidates for many internal positions and roles – even today. Organizations can expand the global reach of recruiting and selection but must also assess the "future" skills and experiences (as cited above). Cultural fit will also become a focal point. In my work with Southeast Asian operations, I have seen workers' adjustment difficulties with American *and* organization-specific cultures. This, too, must be considered. As we look to select for both today and tomorrow, the jobs of managers and Human Resources will become more complex.

RIC'S TAKE ON SELECTING TALENT

Jeff has outlined the importance and complexity of the recruiting, interviewing, and selection processes. I like to tell participants in my formal classroom leadership development courses that hiring the right people for a job is the most critical responsibility they have…and the most impactful. I tell them that if they hire the right people with the right skills and values for the right jobs to complement the right processes, supporting the proper outcomes for our clients and customers, they have conquered 80 percent of the challenges they will face as leaders. As the reader can see, lots of "rights" are implied here and require much effort and thought.

However, the reality of our current environment is that the "right" talent is in limited supply in our labor markets. Unfortunately, we have witnessed the most significant decline in the skills and capabilities of our educational institutions' graduates in U.S. history. There are several underlying causes of this decline, and we will not attempt to diagnose the ailments of our educational system and processes. However, the knowledge and skills gap has become painfully apparent, particularly for the post-Generation X population. As leaders, we must be aware of this gap and do all we can to select the best talent we can find for our open positions while placing more emphasis on our onboarding and ongoing skill development processes.

Given the limited supply of qualified and capable talent in our markets, we must prioritize, streamline, and reinforce the critical nature of the recruiting, interviewing, and selection processes to compete effectively. Gone are the days of scheduling multiple interviews with multiple interviewers for the same candidates. I have witnessed three and 4-month delays in interviewing well-qualified candidates. When those delays exist in the process, the best candidates will find other opportunities to pursue. Multiple interviews with multiple interviewers over an extended period directly reflect a culture consumed with fear and indecision, offering capable, intellectually talented applicants little opportunity for success and job satisfaction. We must also recognize that we rarely can attract talent with all the knowledge, skills, and aptitudes we desire for every vacant position. This challenge underscores the importance of having strong onboarding, learning and development, and career resources and capabilities in our organizations.

3. Developing the Talent – *Learning to Whack the Moles with Impact*:

JEFF DISCUSSES TRAINING AND DEVELOPMENT

According to a recent article from Josh Bersin (2023), corporations spent $340 billion on training. Training is one of the few organizational functions not required to demonstrate cost-benefit or Return on Investment. This chapter will demonstrate that much training wastes money and typically produces no behavior or performance change back on the job.

I once trained government managers and supervisors for a local training company. Overall, my participant "satisfaction" scores were on the lower end. This concerned me, as my evaluation scores were higher in other venues. I discussed my concern with the CEO of the training company, and she told me something quite interesting. She said that, while advocating for learning to occur in the sessions, she realized that some attendees were "required" to attend, whether they wanted to or not, and likely were more interested in being entertained than in learning. She suggested there are two types of trainers – "educators" and "edutainers." The former was there to educate, the latter to educate *and* entertain – and those were the ones who received high satisfaction rating scores. While I ensure my training is participatory and engaging, I am not the Jimmy Kimmel of training.

Think about how you were taught to drive a car. If you did it the "corporate way," you would start with a "warm-up" discussion – "if you were a car, what type of car would you be?" Then, you would have a presentation on how to drive a car – with PowerPoint slides. Next would be a video on the dangers of driving a car (with those high school films from the state police). Finally, you would do a simulation of driving on your X-Box. Of course, this is NOT how you learned to perform skills such as driving a car. Imagine your brain surgeon being trained the "corporate" way.

Training knowledge and skill application on the job is not complicated, but it may take longer than a half day. (By the way, where did we come to the belief that a half-day is an appropriate time to train someone?) If I had been taught to drive a car in four hours, my dad would never have let me drive *his* vehicle. However, we somehow expect employees to apply complex content covered in that amount of time back on the job *without* their manager's support.

So, we continue to "train" employees quickly with often dull and ineffective presentations and media. They get bored and inattentive. Starting as a trainer, I learned to "stimulate" (that is, wake up) participants with sugar and caffeine every 90 minutes. Feed them donuts, cookies, and coffee at breaks; they may return refreshed and ready to learn. Obviously, that is a poor substitute for well-designed instruction and effective development methods.

I understood the role of training accepted by executives and managers – that training (presentations with PowerPoint slides included) would solve individual, team, or organizational performance problems. Most senior managers I have worked with seem to honestly know that the training won't solve their problems – but they invest in it anyway. The fundamental role of training is to impart knowledge and skills to workers to improve their job performance, usually through behavioral change. As I cited in my *Training* magazine article "*Let's Get Rid of the Training Department*" (1988), employers don't want well-trained employees; they want employees who do their jobs well. Training won't necessarily enable them to do that. We only provide training when we are convinced that poor performance is due to a lack of skills or, knowledge, or practice – not other factors in the workplace. An analogy attributed to instructional development guru Robert Mager is to put a gun to a performer's head and ask them to perform a task (don't try this at home or in the workplace). If they do, they do not need training. As Mager states in *Making Instruction Work* (1988),

"Though it often seems hard to believe, instructors are frequently asked to build courses to teach people what they already know or how to use instruction to solve problems that can't be solved by instruction."

In his classic paper, *"When We Teach, What Gets Learned? Today's Crisis in Corporate Training"* (1990), Paul Whitmore describes the evolution of today's primary instructional mode – the presentation. As Whitmore explains, after book printing was invented in the Middle Ages, most people couldn't read, so those who could read gathered the townspeople together and read to them from a book. Today's "presentation" mode of instruction is a modernized carry-over from the Middle Ages. I read (from the PowerPoint slides), and you listen. We do an end-of-class evaluation called the "smile sheet" that measures participant "satisfaction" with the training. Many participants are more satisfied with this type of evaluation since there is often no expectation on the part of the participant (or their manager) to do anything more than listen and enjoy. That's why "edutainers" (as mentioned before) get such high evaluation scores. *Whack!*

Surveys show that most training in organizations is essentially worthless. People don't like it (hence, edutainers). Managers see little value in it. They don't usually improve on-the-job performance. Popular training metrics are generally not tied to strategic business needs or outcomes. In my previous role as a training director for a large corporation, our required metrics for the Training and Development function were the average number of people enrolled in classes and the total number of people actively "participating" in courses during the budget year. While these metrics kept us busy (and politically safe), they had no bearing on what people learned in these classes or if they applied the learning back on the job.

Training (aka Learning and Development – L&D) must change in the fast-changing environment and marketplace. It must impart knowledge and skills and help managers guide their employees to apply skills on the job. A partnership between L&D professionals and managers is required to do this. Higher-level leaders must ensure that managers have the resources (especially the time) to make this happen. Large group instruction and long presentations will become a thing of the past (Middle Ages). Learning and development will become individualized – each person has a training and development plan tied directly to current and anticipated organizational skill and knowledge demands. As mentioned in another chapter, the future focus of learning will be on building new skills ("upskilling") and developing capacity or potential. Changes in technology and the explosion of artificial intelligence (AI) will require employee "reskilling" to keep them current with the skills needed for the job changes. "Edutainers" must go into stand-up comedy or TV talk shows (how about a reality show?) to preserve their skills. One note of caution is that as we transition to individualized learning, self-instructional virtual learning is mainly presented with short-term information recall in quizzes. It is difficult to learn skills via virtual training, as there is little opportunity for the learner to ask questions to clarify or gain additional insight into the learning content, little feedback on information retention, no skills training, no coaching, and likely no reinforcement back on the job. Virtual self-paced training is often a means for cutting back on the greater costs of classroom training. We have gone from four-hour presentations by an edutainer to one-hour virtual presentations with cartoons.

LEADERSHIP WHACK-A-MOLE

Jobs are changing as well. Jobs will move from highly structured to agile, flexible roles. As mentioned in an earlier section, we will hire and promote not for formal education and degrees but for the potential to learn skills needed for the organization's strategic future. This helps explain why learning will become more individualized. We will need a way to prepare employees and managers for specific assignments, projects, and positions. This is the development aspect of talent management. The development will focus more on mentored experiences that prepare people for new roles (for example, job rotation, managing projects with networked teams, and training others (peer training)). The Center for Creative Leadership's research (McCall et al.,1988) on the success factors in moving into an executive management position found that formal training is a very small contributing factor. Experiences, even ones that don't go well, are significant as long as you learn from them. The role of managers will change from the "controller" of tasks and teams to guiding employees to develop their potential in the best interests of the organization and the employees. Technical competence will no longer be a primary factor in job promotion. We're entering the age of redeployment where an "administrative assistant" with relevant skills for an assignment or project may be deployed to work in another way that takes full advantage of their unique set of skills. We'll also find that some senior managers don't possess the skills or capabilities to lead the business into the future and may need to redeploy to other positions or leave the organization.

RIC'S THOUGHTS ON DEVELOPING THE TALENT

As conveyed in Chapter 2, which focuses on developing leadership skills, effective learning occurs on the job with consistent, timely, and focused feedback from a qualified coach, mentor, and supportive supervisor. In that chapter, we outlined various strategies for supporting individual development in the *"Guide to Alternative Development Methods"* (Shriver, 2010) with an assessment of the degree of effectiveness for each of the methods outlined. Another key factor to be considered, in addition to determining the methods used for development, is time. As outlined in several chapters in our book, the rate of change in our environment and within the markets that our businesses are supporting has grown exponentially. With the constancy of rapidly changing market conditions and customer/client expectations in mind, we can no longer rely on traditional textbook learning methodologies that have dominated corporate learning for many years. Most importantly, as leaders, we need to be able to prioritize the importance of the skill and knowledge in question while assessing the potential Return on Investment achieved through the expenditure of time and resources being considered for development.

Current trends in our marketplaces and how the emerging workforce's expectations are voiced call for a very different corporate training and development function. Effective development professionals will assume more of a consultative role as they work with the various functional leaders of the enterprise to help them address strategic and functional gaps in performance. Development professionals must have a thorough knowledge of the business, have a high level of respect for, if not experience in, process improvement, and stay abreast of current learning trends with deference to tried and true adult learning ***principles***. Astute development professionals will fully understand that, in many of the consultations they engage in with the functional leaders of the organization, formal training will be a less emphasized solution. Instead, the development professional must be aware of and ready to engage other enterprise experts in quality, customer service, human resources, engineering, and financial functions to provide holistic solutions to complex problems. While the role of the "edutainer" may not completely vanish, enterprise leaders will expect that the investments made in the formal training and development functions can produce evidence-based, objective results regarding behavioral changes and the key performance indicators for the business. These trends support and reinforce the rapidly expanding role of the Organizational Development professional versus the role of "corporate trainer."

When formal training is needed, professionals I interact with typically need "just-in-time" training - specific, efficient, easy-to-follow, and easily comprehended instructional delivery provided in a usable, easily accessible format within a very short time. This is particularly true for technical, clinical, or administrative tasks that may need to be repeated later, hence the need to have the instructional materials/resources available in an easily accessible "library" or shared digital site (like a Learning Management System (LMS), Teams, SharePoint, etc.). In a corporate setting, it is crucial to have a system-wide infrastructure that grants access to complex procedural and process information to authorized individuals having the necessary security credentials. Development infrastructure primarily relates to the type of Learning Management System in place. In today's world, there is no need to spend millions of dollars on complex HRIS (Human Resource Information System) or LMS systems when there are cloud-based, accessible leasing options available from numerous robust vendors.

LEADERSHIP WHACK-A-MOLE

JEFF LIKES COACHING – A CRITICAL SKILL FOR THE FUTURE

We have referenced the need for ongoing performance feedback and coaching as the most impactful and beneficial way to reinforce targeted learning for individuals and teams. However, what you may be wondering is how the focus on regular, consistent coaching and feedback correlates with the traditional, annual performance review and appraisal processes that have been baked into our human resources policies and structures. This is mostly to appease the corporate legal departments as the best way to combat potential future federal or state regulatory charges or, worse yet, formal lawsuits and unwanted settlement costs. So, let's examine this quandary by reviewing how best to observe, assess, coach, and document employee performance.

Coaching is popular today in the workplace and will become even more prevalent and necessary in the future. Coaching provides a means for helping employees and teams perform their jobs - and accomplish their objectives – successfully. In addition, coaching helps individuals prepare for promotional opportunities and career progression. Mentoring is another means for future development, often for a specific position. In my experience, most in-house coaching involves individual performers and focuses on specific skills or job tasks.

With the advent of networks and cross-functional team environments, along with strategic knowledge and skill-set changes, leaders must ensure that employees and managers are equipped to deploy this new knowledge and skill set into practice. This will require well-designed training and coaching by managers and leaders. Executive and senior leaders will also need coaching skills to help subordinate leaders and staff become more knowledgeable about organizational design, strategic thinking, adapting to shifting markets and environments, and many other skills. New skills and behaviors for top leaders will also be needed. As the command-and-control style fades, new leadership styles that reshape how leaders lead will emerge.

Companies are reassessing the need for external coaches versus internal managers and peer coaches. Executives will require expert outside coaching to learn much of the knowledge and skills mentioned in the paragraph above and for personal adaptation and behavior change needed to lead in their new roles. Too often, external coaching engagements turn into personal "therapy" or "life coaching" sessions, allowing leaders to express their frustrations. Such engagements do not typically produce long-term changes in behavior or decision-making capability. In my consulting practice, I have often been asked to coach someone who needs "fixing" (i.e., being seen as the cause of a problem). This should not be the role of a coach. Instead, it is the responsibility of the manager.

Many organizations have initiated manager and peer coaching with established skill training programs. Recognizing that employees and managers have a great deal of knowledge and skill to impart, intra-team or cross-functional coaching is a way to develop people without the cost of outside consultants. In addition, internal coaches already know the culture and practices of the organization.

Middle managers cannot coach their team members in all the skills and behaviors needed to perform their tasks since they don't necessarily possess those skills themselves. Instead, the role of the manager-coach will be to guide the development of their team members to promotional positions or in preparation for working on a network or cross-functional project team. Peer coaching will supplement the manager's role, whereby frontline employees across the organization will coach, support, and reinforce needed skills. Training can teach managers and project team members the skills and processes to do such coaching. How leaders and peers coach the members of our various teams is critical. While we do not intend to comprehensively address the skill and the "art" of coaching in this book, Ric will outline some key steps and considerations for anyone engaged in a coaching role below.

RIC OFFERS TIPS FOR JUST-IN-TIME COACHING OPPORTUNITIES

I have outlined below some key steps and criteria I have utilized for effective one-on-one coaching opportunities:

- Determine the reason for and ultimate purpose or desired outcome of the coaching. If the outcome is ***irrelevant to the business***, then decide not to engage in a coaching conversation.

- Based on a relevant purpose and desired outcome for the coaching, determine what, where, and how you should provide the coaching following the general guidance offered below:

- If the coaching is to correct inappropriate behavior, incorrect task completion, or insufficient or incorrect communication, it should be done almost immediately after being observed preferably in private. During this type of coaching, the emphasis should be on the observed (or reported by credible witnesses) behavior, task, or communication, followed by a question or questions to validate the observed or reported behavior(s). In any intervention focused on immediate correction, you, as the leader, should allow the employee to offer their rationale and/or perceptions of why the undesirable behavior, action, or communication occurred. However, for the most part, you, as the leader, should do most of the talking, emphasizing gaining agreement with the coached employee for immediate improvement and correction.

- If the coaching is to help an individual problem solve, troubleshoot, or address a work-related dilemma, you should ensure that adequate time is blocked to provide the coaching. This type of coaching should initially involve more observation and questioning, followed by potential direction or demonstration by you or an experienced and capable team member.

- If the coaching discusses individual development related to the employee's career aspirations or personal growth, ensure that adequate time, preferably away from the immediate work area, is scheduled. This type of coaching should emphasize open-ended questions, active listening, and joint agreement on the career path or personal growth avenues. Your support and potential future involvement with the team member's plans should be clarified and confirmed.

- If the coaching recognizes an individual's performance and contribution to the business and team, provide that recognition as soon as possible after observing the performance or contribution… for this type of coaching, do it publicly for the full team to appreciate the individual.

Regardless of the type of coaching being offered, follow-up should occur within a reasonable timeframe to ensure that the coached employee or peer is committed to the corrected behavior, problem resolution, or career/personal growth direction agreed upon.

4. A Successful and Impactful Performance Review Process – *Monitoring Performance and Feedback – Moles Considered*

Performance appraisals are historically unpopular. They are typically ineffective assessments of human performance in our workplaces. This section will help you understand the causes of this ineffectiveness and why it occurs. You'll learn methods for less subjective, more valid statistical and non-statistical appraisals. You'll see a possible new paradigm for assessing employee performance.

RIC'S STRUGGLES WITH PERFORMANCE APPRAISAL AND REVIEW PROCESSES

In an earlier chapter segment, I described the first "performance review" tool I was exposed to as an early leader in a traditional "Personnel Department." The tool was simple, easy to administer, and could be applied to all members of the organization's team without much thought. The one thing it did was foster simple, direct feedback and communication around readily observable behaviors that either worked for or against the organization's mission, vision, and values. However, despite the simplicity of this tool, everyone hated having to deal with the burden of conducting annual performance reviews. Moreover, I was the evil HR guy who was tasked with ensuring everyone received a formal performance review that was ultimately signed, acknowledged, and carefully inserted into the official personnel file housed in our "Personnel Department"– ugh!

Not much has changed with the perceptions leaders and staff have of the performance review process. However, most of the performance review process is now housed in a digital, human capital management/human resources information system environment. Throughout my career, I have tried on many occasions to involve the leaders and staff of the organizations I have worked with in designing and developing more effective, relevant, and focused performance review tools. Those design and development initiatives have produced tools and processes that were initially received well. Unfortunately, after the "honeymoon" period of introduction, the reaction of leaders and staff has been typically the same – "Ugh – do we have to do this again?! What a pain in the butt!"

What I have learned about the performance review process is that the tool for review must be simple, easy to understand, and *related directly to the work that the individual being appraised is doing* in the organization. However, more importantly, the tool and process should focus on future development, providing a mechanism for clearly identifying and documenting specific developments that will enhance the knowledge, skills, and abilities of all members of the team. The extent to which organizations can systematically inventory, categorize, and prioritize the requested development opportunities will drive real performance improvement.

LEADERSHIP WHACK-A-MOLE

In a recent role as the corporate leader of Learning and Organizational Development, I worked with a multi-disciplinary group of leaders and staff to produce a tool and process that initially relied on the accurate assessment of one's ability to perform the essential duties of their job "with or without reasonable accommodation." There is no Likert scale rating (1932) for this assessment, only a "yes" or "no" response with supporting documentation for a "no" response. Of course, this initial assessment heavily depends on accurate, relevant, and timely job descriptions being available, understood, and accepted by those being evaluated – often a daunting task, as we have previously discussed in this chapter dealing with job design and descriptions.

Another universally accepted assessment focuses on consistently demonstrating behaviors supporting the organization's primary values. These values were developed and well-documented through a highly credible process that a former Chief Human Resources Officer had facilitated a few years earlier. As with the essential duty assessment outlined above, a simple "yes" or "no" response is expected from both the self-evaluation and the manager's evaluation, with documentation requested in support of "no" responses. For the first and second portions of the evaluation process, an option exists within the tool for initiating "peer reviews and feedback" from leader-endorsed peers.

The final and most crucial element of the performance review process is the section focused on desired education and development. This section emphasizes what each team member can do to improve performance and add value to the organization's mission, vision, values, and desired outcomes. For leaders in the organization, this requires a well-structured process to ensure that "S.M.A.R.T." (Doran, 1981) development goals are designed, documented, and aligned with the organization's strategic priorities.

For those readers who are not familiar with the term "S.M.A.R.T." goals (Doran, ibid.), the definition emphasizes the importance of goals being 1) **S**pecific, 2) **M**easurable, 3) **A**ctionable and **A**ttainable, 4) **R**elevant to the Mission, Vision, Values, and Key Performance Indicators of the Department/Unit and Organization, and finally 5) **T**ime-based within a realistic time.

The challenge with the tools and process outlined above is that the organization's leadership must take the practice seriously by dedicating ample time and effort to the implementation and completion of the process. Suppose the organization's senior leadership does not expect and reinforce this practice. Consequently, leaders are obligated to shoulder a necessary burden, prioritizing the satisfaction of clients and customers who expect top-notch results from the provided services and products. In all the industries that Jeff and I have worked in, we have seen and experienced many obstacles inhibiting the focus and dedication to the performance review and development process that could and should have been in place.

One of the biggest obstacles I have experienced throughout my career is the "span of control" challenge. Many department leaders have more than 100 individuals reporting directly to them, making meaningful performance reviews and development discussions impossible. From my observations, this span of control issue exists for two key reasons: 1) staffing and productivity restrictions and 2) the fragmented nature of leadership roles and associated accountabilities within the organization. I can recall on many occasions how the demand from senior leadership to "hit your productivity" targets derailed legitimate efforts to honestly assess and develop performance by necessitating spans of control that made those efforts impossible. The second reason directly impacts the leader's ability to positively affect the performance of supervised individuals and teams through targeted, specific feedback related to their assigned roles and responsibilities. The following section will address this critical need and the perceived gap focused on performance review and development processes and tools.

JEFF EXPANDS ON THE PROBLEMS WITH FORMAL PERFORMANCE REVIEWS

Surveys have recognized for years that neither managers nor employees like traditional performance appraisals, especially reviews. They are an icon of years gone by. First developed as a method to evaluate military recruits in the 1920s, we continue to use them today (with their *shiny new object* packages). Why do so many people dislike them? Let's look:

Here we go again. It's time for the annual performance appraisal review. Don't get me wrong, I don't dislike having my performance appraised – it's just how it's done. I appreciated the feedback on my performance – as long as it was accurate and non-biased. In most of my jobs, the review was primarily about my salary increase (since salary increases were tied to appraisal ratings). Perform "well" and expect a 4.0 out of 5.0 rating. The 4.0 rating was the goal of most of my peers since 5.0 ratings were virtually impossible to achieve (as a part of the organization's culture). So, one of the reasons people dislike performance appraisals is that they are often tied to compensation. The name of the game is maximizing the appraisal score you receive, hence maximizing the salary increase. This influences performance by the employees doing the things that will get them the greatest payout, not necessarily for achieving the goals defined last year or the requirements in the job description. Knowing the subjectivity and biases built into the appraisal system, employees learn quickly what behaviors will get them the best scores. Subjectivity and bias are the other reasons that employees dislike performance appraisals.

I was never always sure why I received the ratings I did on my appraisals. Throughout the year, I did those things that I believed would maximize my rating (and, consequently, my income): maintained positive relations with my team members and managers, behaved consistently with the culture, and got the job done! However, the reviews were always subjective, sometimes based to a degree on my manager's feelings about me and whether I met their (stated and unstated) expectations. As a manager, I was aware of my power to "influence" appraisal scores and narratives. The subjectivity of performance appraisals allowed me to reward and punish employees if I chose to.

There was little validity in performance appraisals – little actual **measurement** of my work. Job responsibility ratings were often subjective, even when **one** relevant example of a performance task was given with the rating. Most of my performance appraisal forms had a section for job responsibilities, with a rating scale and blank space for a brief narrative or example to explain the rating. These, too, were subjective, as one example does not make for a valid or reliable rating. It also presumes that the manager has documentation or measurement (or a great memory) of my performance over the appraisal **year**. The form itself may have no place for extra-responsibility projects – those not on the job responsibilities section of the form (and which may be as or more important to the business as my job functions). Still, of all the appraisal sections, the job responsibilities section may be the best indicator of actual job performance - if it is visible to the manager consistently.

Now, let's talk about appraising traits. What does it mean to possess "integrity" or "professionalism?" Traits, unless clearly defined and understood in the appraisal, are nebulous and open to interpretation. What exactly would I show to demonstrate *integrity*? What behavior would I demonstrate? Not knowing these things at the beginning of the appraisal period leaves me at a disadvantage at review time. How about being a "team player?" According to management expert Patrick Lencioni (2002), effective team members will initiate and engage in "healthy" conflict with their teammates. Would my "team player" rating increase if I followed Lencioni's advice? I don't think so, particularly if our culture frowns upon any conflict within the team. I might be tagged as a troublemaker (which may lower my appraisal score).

In the 1990s, 360-degree (or "multi-rater") performance reviews became popular in the workplace (the model was developed for the German military around 1930). This Flavor-of-the-Month "shiny new object" was the latest version of performance appraisal. It wasn't much better than the one-on-one boss-employee appraisal. Having six additional superiors, peers, and subordinates subjectively rate you doesn't improve the *validity* of the ratings. While rater comments may be helpful, they are still subjective and open to rater bias. Consequently, having six people appraise your "integrity" doesn't make the results more objective. 360s can be used for political purposes to affect the score (and perhaps the promotion) of the individual being appraised. In a recent webinar, one of the hosts described 360 appraisals as "fun." I can't remember anyone ever using that word to describe 360s. Mine weren't by any means! *Whack!*

Performance appraisal must be more objective in order to be valid and reliable. In my 40 years of consulting, I have seen only a handful of large businesses use objective and valid approaches. Some large corporations that implemented Total Quality Management, Six Sigma, or Lean *didn't* always measurably appraise performance.

A problem with subjective appraisals is that they are not motivating. Sometimes, the employee can't identify the causes of the ratings ("good" or "bad"). Motivation comes from seeing that your successful work (effort) leads directly to an expected outcome or result (Vroom's Expectancy Theory). When a performer isn't clear about what they did to "earn" their ratings, then motivation is stifled. If I don't know what I did this year to get the ratings I did, then how will I know what to do next year? As a manager, when I have a dozen or more reviews to write in a short amount of (limited) time, my recollection of your performance (because I likely do not have measurable data to use) and behavior may be skewed. (On a side note, I received a quarterly achievement award from my company and was never told what I did to earn it. I wondered what I needed to do to get another award.)

"Forced Ranking" is another problematic practice in appraising performance. In Forced Ranking, ratings are distributed on a bell curve, with the bottom 10 percent of the ranked employees likely losing their jobs. This practice encourages competition (and sometimes political behavior) on the part of the team members, all of whom fight to keep their jobs. The belief behind this practice is that employees will be better motivated to perform within the top 90 percent. Collaboration can be harmed if I hope to keep my job at your expense. The problem with Forced Ranking is that if all your team members perform "well," some will still be let go. This will occur year after year, and the team and organization will lose much knowledge and experience. In companies I am familiar with that used Forced Ranking, I have seen chronic anxiety and fear among employees that they may lose their (usually high-paying, professional) jobs.

Another problem with subjective appraisals is "equity," or fairness. For example, you and I are co-workers. You don't work very hard and make a lot of errors. I, on the other hand, am a superb worker. My work is always on time, complete, and error-free. I am a hard worker. I often pick up your slack when you do unfinished and error-filled work. Upon leaving the boss's office today, where you received your annual performance review, you walked by my cubicle to tell me you got a 4.0 (out of 5.0) overall rating. After congratulating you, it's my turn to see the boss for my review. Of course, comparing myself to you – a slacker – I certainly expect to get a rating of 5.0. During the review discussion, my manager couldn't say enough good things about me and my performance – including how I help you get your work done. So, my manager tells me he is "awarding" me a rating of 4.0. *Whack!* I do twice as much as you, twice as well, and even do your work, and I get the same rating (and percentage salary increase) as you! That's not fair; that's what *equity* is all about. So, what do you think I'll be doing over the next year? Working my tail off? Helping you out? I think not. Now I'm pissed and demotivated. Why not just sit on my ass and do little? I will still likely get only a 4.0 rating next year. Alternatively, I may look for a new job where they appreciate my efforts and compensate me equitably. So, you see how performance appraisals can affect work equity (fairness) and, hence, lower morale and motivation.

These problems with performance appraisals have bothered me for many years. I have worked tirelessly to help businesses make theirs more objective and constructive. However, I found very few business owners or executives interested in making such a change.

Why? Developing, implementing, and managing such a system takes much work, and "we don't have the time." "We know what you're saying makes sense, **but** we've always done it this way," or "It's too difficult to measure performance."

Quality improvement guru W. Edwards Deming (1986) believed that 85 percent of performance failure is due to deficiencies in the systems and process rather than with the employee. He said the role of management is to change the process rather than badger individuals to do better. Consequently, managers have some responsibility for work outcomes, as they influence the means and ends of work. As Deming says, "Put a good person in a bad system, and the bad system wins, no contest." As he suggested, employees have limited control over their performance, but management does!

In 1994, I wrote an article titled *"Appraise the Performance System...Not the Performer,"* which describes using an objective "appraisal" system. The system's analysis tools have long been used for "root" problem identification. The article demonstrates that traditional performance appraisal doesn't always address the root causes of performance. Read a summary of the article below:

Individuals are a part of a **holistic** performance 'system' in which they operate. We can demonstrate this in the following "cause-and-effect" diagram:

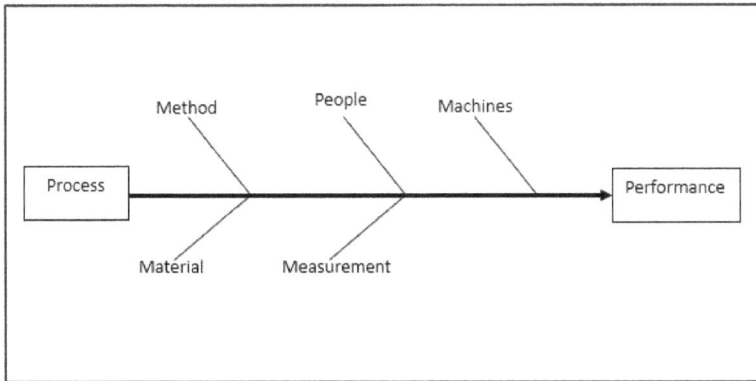

Figure 4.1. The Problem Analysis (Cause and Effect) Model (Adapted from Ishikawa, 1990)

The cause-and-effect analysis examines a 5-factor domain where the root-cause problem may occur. Looking at this cause-and-effect diagram, we can see m a n y possible 'causes' of performance success or failure.

Applying the cause-and-effect model to performance appraisal shows that the individual performer (people) depends on methods, materials, machines, and measurements to perform their job successfully. All these elements of the cause-and-effect diagram represent a performance system. Appraising a performer without appraising the other parts of the system is like diagnosing a car's poor performance by checking only the battery - you look at only one part of the system.

Traditional performance appraisal focuses primarily on the individual performer, not the performance system. To use the car analogy, we "appraise" the battery when the real causes of performance deficiency may be an error on the driver's part or a problem with the onboard computer. Using the cause-and- effect diagram, we can demonstrate Deming's "85/15" principle:

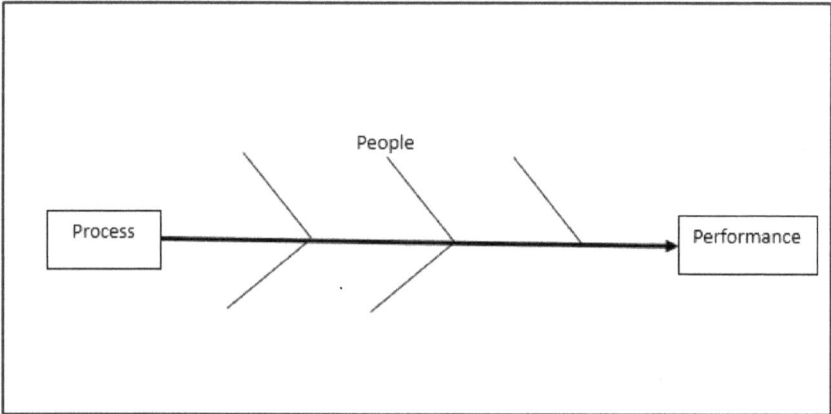

Figure 4.2. When Only People Are Appraised

Figure 4.2 shows that traditional performance appraisal holds the performer 100 percent responsible for the performance and disregards the methods, materials, measurement, and machines. In conventional performance appraisal, we miss *many* possible causes of performance. However, "goals" or "development" activities are precisely what we assign in traditional performance appraisals to improve the performance of workers (as managers sometimes say, "send them for training").

To "correct" performance appraisals, we must appraise the *entire performance system,* not just the performer!

Performance system appraisal uses problem analysis methods (like cause-and-effect diagramming) to identify the "root causes" of performance.

LEADERSHIP WHACK-A-MOLE

By appraising the performance system, we can pinpoint and resolve the root causes, thereby identifying the sources of performance. The "key" to performance system appraisal is gathering the "right" information about how the system achieves its output. This means that all relevant information sources must be included.

Our model for performance system appraisal is the model for cause-and-effect problem analysis. Although this model is used extensively to improve the performance of our work processes and systems, management has had difficulty translating its use to performance appraisal and improvement. Our management paradigm views individual workers as the locus of control over their work. Consequently, they overlook many root causes of performance problems.

As noted before, to implement a "quick fix," we revised our performance appraisal systems to conduct "360-degree" appraisals, in which superiors, peers, and subordinates appraise the performer. The fallacy of 360-degree appraisal is that it is irrelevant how many people appraise the performer when the performer themself is only one element in the performance system. No matter how many people appraise, they still must appraise the performance system - not the performer. Consequently, a group of appraisers tells us that the battery (to use our car analogy) is the problem. When we apply performance system appraisal, we no longer "point the finger" at the performers for problem causes beyond their control. Or, as Dr. Deming described, "driving fear out of the workplace." Now, we can engage the performer (and the rest of the 360-degree team) in a collaborative partnership to identify the root causes of performance.

Such collaboration frees workers to focus their energy and creativity on improving work processes and procedures rather than self-protection and maximizing compensation. It's time to throw away those "traditional" performance review forms and begin appraising the performance system - not just the performer.

So, where are we now? It's been 50 years since Total Quality Management popularized performance analysis - over that time, we have applied various forms. However, there has been little application of these models in the workplace. It's time to update our performance evaluation methods.

With fast-moving change coming to organizations, work will be moving from the individual to networked teams from multiple functional areas of the organization. As noted earlier in this chapter, significant changes are occurring even today in how we design jobs and select and appraise "talent." The effect on performance measurement and management will be substantial. The manager's role will shift from the hierarchical controller to a coach to guide their team members to work effectively in networked (cross-functional) teams. An appraisal will require multi-directional information (feedback) to allow the manager to evaluate performance more accurately. Criteria for performance will change. Job requirements will enlarge to include skill sets needed to perform in a lean, agile workplace.

Managers functioning as coaches will enable more consistent, constant, and measurable information to their team members rather than only through annual or quarterly reviews. This will require information flow and connectivity with the network, project teams, and other functional managers. Some companies use shorter-term discussions with their employees rather than formal annual or quarterly reviews. In the previous segment of this chapter, we offered some coaching tips for leaders who need "just-in-time" interventions with members of their respective teams when behavioral or outcome expectations are not being met. Often held weekly, team members can have real-time conversations about the employee's performance. With the shifting emphasis on future-oriented knowledge and skills, these discussions will also focus on the employee's development into greater "strategic" positions, adapting to the organization's culture, and understanding the organization's vision and strategies. Companies like Zappos (Hsieh, 2010) have used a Holacracy model (Robertson, 2015), where employees create ad-hoc teams to solve problems – without the direction (or involvement) of formal managers.

Business and work are going in a new direction, and our current performance appraisal processes must catch up. In the highest performing, most adaptable enterprises, teams focused on key initiatives, projects, or organizational challenges will provide constructive, objective feedback to each other. This ensures that the knowledge, skills, and abilities needed to successfully support them are continuously enhanced through open, transparent, and honest communication.

5. Understanding and Dealing with Performance Problems – *When the Moles Incite Undesirable Performance*

JEFF LOOKS AT IMPROVING PERFORMANCE PROBLEMS

In the ideal school, all students get straight A's (using a criteria-based, not normative, approach). In the perfect workplace, all employees meet or exceed performance standards. Of course, this is not reality. Workers' performance outcomes can show a wide range of results. When those results and expectations do not meet standards, we may have a "performance problem" – mainly if the problem is chronic. In my career, I saw that most employee performance "problems" resulted in some corrective action – typically a "Performance Improvement Plan" or PIP. The employee in question receives the PIP, a "contract" developed by the manager to help the employee correct their subpar performance. When a PIP is introduced into the corrective action process, the employee can see it as either constructive or punishing. Too often, I have seen the PIP used as a punishment tool ("up to and including termination"). I have witnessed PIPs that set up the employees to fail in order to terminate them. I know this because, as a consultant, I have observed this firsthand. Despite the ethical and legal issues, this is an often-used practice in management. I have been consulted too many times about how to "fix" an employee or a manager. Often, the person doesn't even know there is a problem.

The other side of a PIP is the constructive one. Managers plan and work with the employee to fix the problem leading to performance discrepancies. Managers may recommend coaching, feedback, problem analysis, or goal setting to improve performance. In such cases, the manager's support is critical to improved performance. I have seen many instances where employees improve performance with the constructive use of PIPs.

DEFINING PERFORMANCE

What is performance? It refers to executing a task or activity to accomplish an end. We sometimes use the term to describe the execution of a set of tasks, such as a project. Our performance expectations are based on standards defining the outcome level. So, we must provide the performer with clear expectations and standards. Otherwise, how can workers be expected to perform successfully if they don't know or understand the standards and outcomes? It's like asking someone to score a hockey goal while blindfolded and without a stick.

Managers often use poor problem analysis when attempting to identify the root cause of a performance problem. Instead of focusing solely on the performer, managers need to consider additional factors in seeking the root cause. Tom Gilbert's PROBE model (1982, used with permission) of performance analysis and improvement provides a holistic approach to identifying and remediating performance problems. PROBE stands for:

Performance: comparing actual results to desired goals or standards.

Resources: access to necessary resources like materials, instructions, and tools to perform the task.

Opportunities: situations that hinder or enable performance.

Behavior: what people are doing or not doing affects the task's outcome.

Environment: external factors that affect performance.

The PROBE model helps us understand the many factors influencing poor performance. The idea that a performer is solely responsible for a performance problem is nonsensical. Without a problem analysis, we can't be sure what the root cause of the problem is. So, often, the individual performer is set up to be the solitary cause of the deficiency.

I worked for a Human Resources organization that used technology to track the employees' performance on various tasks. They were required to log client visit information. This was difficult because there were no instructions on using the system during onboarding, the program was quite complicated, and the performance standards were unrealistic (100 percent accuracy and completeness of each entry). They had difficulty learning and using the system and consequently got "dinged" by their boss on their performance reviews for not meeting performance standards. Fortunately, they didn't receive a PIP. A new manager had taken over their department and dropped the performance standards altogether. *Whack!*

Performance discrepancies (problems) cannot be entirely avoided, particularly if the cause of the problem is not the performer. To solve the problem, we must start with a "performance analysis." There are various types of performance analysis models – all of which help to identify the causes of the problem. In this way, the root causes of the problem can be identified and remediated. This approach is more effective than a PIP because it looks at the whole performance "system" – not just the performer.

We begin by identifying the expected results of the performance (or task). This is defined in the goals and standards for the performance. The problem, then, is the deviation from the goals and standards. Practically, the performer is expected to produce 100 widgets a day but averages only 75. The discrepancy is that 25 widgets were not made, but we still don't know the cause of the problem. We can attribute the cause to the performer, but that may be a misdiagnosis. So, the next step is to find the causes of the problem.

There are many performance analysis tools and methods available that can help locate the root causes. I'll illustrate an analysis model using a diagram from my *Performance Planner* (Fierstein, 1994) in Figure 4.3.

1. Successful performance (diagrammed on the right) is affected by several factors on the left, shown as Performer, Job, and Environment. Any elements within those factors can also affect the achievement of the performance.

2. For example, a performer cannot perform as expected. While developing skills may compensate for the lack of ability, sometimes it cannot. We can punish the performers all we want, but they probably won't be able to perform as expected. That explains why I don't play basketball for the Chicago Bulls (and why parents should not say, "You can be *anything* you want to be" - because you *can't*.)

3. The job itself may be the reason that performance is not as expected. Faulty job design, standards, processes, or

feedback can directly impact performance. If any of these are the root cause, then the performer may be unable to meet expectations. I previously mentioned that the unrealistic job standards (100% complete and accurate for every entry) led to "dings" in performance reviews. The manager was unwilling and unable to change the standards.

4. The environment can have many obstacles to successful performance. As shown in the model below, my performance can be affected by a lack of – or poor quality - resources, incentives, and rewards (I get punished for doing as expected or rewarded for not meeting expectations). In my career, an organizational barrier I faced was the company culture, whose values differed from mine.

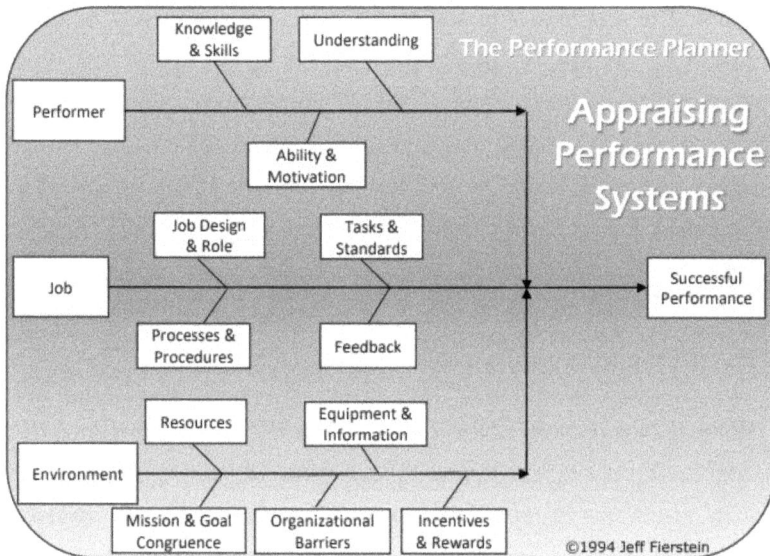

Figure 4.3. The Performance Planner

Placing cause on the performer without doing a performance analysis is a great way to lose the trust and respect of your subordinates – or even have them quit. Let's hear from Ric about his experience dealing with performance problems.

RIC'S TURNAROUND STORY - AN OPPORTUNITY FOR PERFORMANCE DIAGNOSIS

I can recall assuming a leadership role during my career where I was told, very early in my tenure with the organization, that one of the professionals on the team I was leading would have to be carefully observed within the initial few weeks following my arrival. I was told that this individual was known for allegedly dodging accountability for the position's expected roles, responsibilities, and outcomes. I was also told that the individual was also allegedly known in the department for their often-light-hearted demeanor, someone who seemed to find humor and laughter amid dealing with department challenges, even if the circumstances surrounding the challenges were serious. As any good manager would do upon assuming the responsibility for the new team, I began finding out what everyone was doing, how they were spending their time, and what kind of results each team member was achieving. This discovery process was particularly important as I reviewed the work of the team member in question.

What I discovered during my conversations with this alleged "low performing" individual was that they had never been given or asked to prepare a current job description or formal operational or development goals. In essence, they had been left alone to do whatever they deemed appropriate or at the request of a senior leader within the organization, in or outside their home department. When I reviewed previous performance reviews completed for this person, they were either "stellar" or reflected that the person was meeting expectations. However, the department leadership was convinced they were a slacker and might need to be replaced with a more responsible, talented person.

Having worked with Jeff in previous years and having been exposed to the nature of actual performance management tools and techniques, I conducted my own diagnosis of the "performance gaps" that my senior leaders were convinced were not worth the time, energy, and resources needed to remedy. As indicated in the preceding paragraphs, I did conduct a thorough assessment of the work that this individual was currently doing compared to the work that, in this role, I expected to be done. With the input and involvement of this person, we were able to prepare a current job description along with some initial expectations for performance in support of the essential duties of the job. Within a few short weeks, it became clear that this person had been neglected by the previous supervisor, who, admittedly, had little or no knowledge of the specialized function that this employee was in. Within the following year, the employee in question rose to assume some additional key responsibilities in support of a significant initiative sponsored by the senior executive over our department. They actively engaged in this initiative and provided countless ideas for improvement and eventual positive organizational impact. Within another year, this person completed a Master's level graduate program and was nominated and chosen for a key leadership role in the state professional organization recognized by their discipline.

In the case outlined in the previous paragraphs, the "duty to produce a desired" outcome algorithm could be applied and followed. The first question in the algorithm for this duty is, "Was the duty to produce an outcome known to the employee?" In this case, the answer to that question was an emphatic "no." Involving this person in an ongoing discussion and initiative to define the appropriate roles, responsibilities, and expected behaviors resulted in corrected performance gaps and some unexpected, positive organizational outcomes. The individual's refocused efforts resulted in clients and customers perceiving increased value being provided by the department.

This turnaround story reflects the importance of the need for more disciplined, structured processes to be in place when leaders are dealing with perceived "performance problems." A relatively simple model I have recently been introduced to lays out three essential duties that should be considered within any reputable performance management process: 1) the duty to avoid causing unjustifiable risk or harm, 2) the duty to follow procedural rules, and

3) the duty to produce desired outcomes. This model also outlines five behaviors that can be observed and documented when completing an objective performance diagnosis: 1) simple human error; 2) at-risk behavior; 3) reckless behavior; 4) knowledgeable, conscious behavior; and 5) purposeful, malicious behavior with the intent to cause harm or damage. The model I describe here calls for the application of logical thought processes, or "algorithms," to carefully answer questions that can enable more objective, logical paths for dealing with the perceived "performance problems." (Just Culture, 2010)

In the next chapter, we will explore the importance of every leader playing a role in the customer/client satisfaction process to support and sustain successful business outcomes.

LESSONS LEARNED

Managing Performance

1. The nature and structure of work is changing. Performance Management remains the same. With changes in technology and required skills (e.g. Artificial Intelligence), we need to revamp the Performance Management system.
2. Job descriptions must change. Defining the current job is not enough. By deemphasizing formal education and credentials and focusing more on skills and capabilities, we can recruit and select candidates with *potential* for redeployment as needed.
3. Do we hire more for skills and experience or culture fit. We have to consider both because both will change. A candidate should be able to "upskill" as well as alter their values and beliefs to accommodate changes in the business' strategies and culture.
4. There are "educators" and "edutainers." Select them carefully. It depends on whether your training outcome is learning or entertaining.
5. Training should be performance-based and applied back on the job versus lengthy informational presentations. Training is used when there is a knowledge or skill deficiency.
6. Training and development must become more individualized to provide upskilling and promotional opportunities tied to the organization's strategy and goals.

LESSONS LEARNED

Managing Performance

7. Coaching will become even more important in the workplace as all employees will be considered for redeployment into jobs that fit the abilities and interests of employees.

8. Traditional performance appraisal is outdated. We must find new ways to evaluate performance.

9. There are many problems with traditional performance appraisal: validity, reliability, equity, trait assessment, 360^0 appraisals, and Forced Ranking.

10. Performance occurs in systems. We have to appraise the system – not the individual performer – to holistically understand what causes performance and performance problems.

Chapter 5

Identifying and Meeting Customer Needs

When the Moles Interfere with Customer Service

CHALLENGE QUESTIONS FOR THE READER:

1. Have you clearly identified your primary customers and their expectations for the product or service?
2. How do you measure your customers' expectations? How do you improve your organization's performance to meet or exceed those expectations?
3. What is your process for regularly assessing and meeting the current needs of your primary customers?
4. Do you have some customers who are not financially profitable to your business? Why do you continue to serve them?

Regardless of our level of leadership in the organization or managing as a sole proprietor, we all have customers and clients whom we must please to succeed. Understanding and accepting our roles with the customer/client focus in mind is a foundational principle to drive our purpose, goals, processes, functions, staffing, scheduling, and allocation of physical and financial resources. In this chapter, we will explain and reinforce the importance of knowing and understanding our customers' needs and expectations and partnering with them to support and develop our enterprise growth and improvement strategies.

JEFF'S METHOD FOR MEETING AND IMPROVING CUSTOMER SATISFACTION

I recently underwent major surgery that laid me up in a hospital bed for a week. While very few of us choose to incur an extended inpatient hospital stay, we are constrained there, and we hope our experience is positive. Overall, I can say that the staff "service" was good, but I experienced several problems. I would have expected those problems to have been resolved previously. There were things like not changing the bed sheets or my hospital gown for the week and the quality and taste of the food. Of course, after discharge, I received a customer satisfaction survey from the hospital. I gave the facility high marks on most questions but cited the abovementioned problems. I wondered how many other former patients cited the sheets, gown, and food problems in earlier surveys. Many, I suspect, had voiced their concerns. Yet nothing was done to fix the problems - to meet the customer's requirements. It's one thing to "measure" customer satisfaction and quite another to implement effective solutions. This chapter looks at just that – how do individual leaders measure and initiate resolution to the issues our customers have brought to their attention, and what should organizations do to support and reinforce the ongoing process of assessing and taking meaningful action from the feedback that is received?

Determining the "correct" customer for your product or service starts with the marketing work described in the business plan (if there is one) at the business's inception. As a leader, you must be fully aware of and involved in the assessment, measurement, and implications of the customers' needs. As the enterprise grows, we can better define the customer base. New or refined products can expand the customer base or reach new customer niches. As a more mature organization, we strategically target markets in our plan. All of this is to say that we must be sure that the target market and customers we select are, in fact, the right ones – that their need matches the function or benefit of our product or service. Innovators like Steve Jobs have transformed the market-need-to-product paradigm by creating products like the iPad and iPhone, for which there seemed to be a premature need (if any actual need at all). We must be clear about who is buying our products and services so that we can design and engineer them to meet the customers' needs, sell them, and generate revenue.

Several methods are used to determine if we are meeting the customer's needs. Perhaps the most informal one is to track sales to see the market activity for our products. This method, however, may not consider whether quality could be improved (and generate greater sales) or if outside factors will drop your sales (for example, new or improved competitor products or economic changes like inflation, interest rates, or public health epidemics like COVID-19). More formal customer surveys provide data on the customer experience and can be used to indicate if customer expectations were met.

As a management consultant, I have seen customer dissatisfaction with products and services. Not all this dissatisfaction came from the product or services provided but rather from performance problems within the business. For example, a manufacturing plant received customer complaints because it failed to deliver orders on time. The problem was not with the product but a manufacturing process that moved too slowly. The customer, of course, doesn't care about the problems in manufacturing. They want the product delivered as agreed to. And if you can't get it there on time, I'll bet your competitors can. Ultimately, the organization's leaders must ensure that a comprehensive and objective process is in place to diagnose the root causes of issues creating customer dissatisfaction and potential migration of customers and clients to a competitor.

In my experience, the most effective method for assuring customer satisfaction is "process management." A business is a "system" with multiple processes that work together to create and deliver products to customers. All processes must be optimized and coordinated to meet a customer's expectations. Because each process has outputs with standards (requirements), those outputs must be defined with measurements to ensure the requirements are met. The business, then, becomes like an "assembly line," where one function leads into another to create a process flow. As shown in Figure 5.1 below, each function's primary process has inputs and outputs that must be met for each function to perform optimally. Although a manufacturing example, the model applies to nonmanufacturing systems as well.

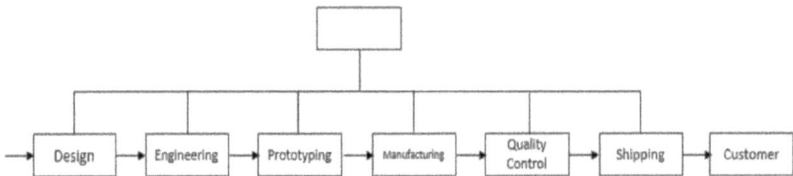

Figure 5.1. Functional "assembly line" as a process flow

A process management method comprises the following steps:

LEADERSHIP WHACK-A-MOLE

1. Identify and quantify the customer's requirements (typically in cost, quality, and schedule).
2. Identify the processes and functions to meet the customer's requirements.
3. Establish a process flow that defines the internal movement of material or services to each function.
4. Each function's process must meet its input requirements for cost, quality, and schedule.
5. Establish an internal communication, monitoring, and measurement structure for each function's inputs and outputs.
6. Measure the effectiveness of each function's outputs to the next function in the flow.
7. Determine gaps or variations in each process and correct them.
8. Repeat steps 1-8 (particularly if customer requirements change).

The functions (i.e. departments) shown in Figure 5.1 demonstrate a process flow that ultimately leads to the customer. Each function produces an output of material or services that becomes an input for the next function in the flow. Therefore, each function has inputs that get transformed into outputs (as indicated by the arrows).

The process flow is designed to make sure that each function produces outputs that meet cost, quality, and schedule requirements. Each internal function must meet the requirements of its internal customer in order to eventually meet the external customer's needs. In this way, we have a pattern of internal "suppliers" and "customers."

For example, using the flowchart in Figure 5.1, the Design department will receive input (from the customer via Sales

Engineering) with specifications for the design of the product. The Design department will have requirements (cost, quality, schedule) that its internal "supplier" must meet for Design to produce a "quality" output for the Engineering function.

I consulted with an aerospace parts manufacturing company, and the Design department was continually frustrated because the customer kept changing the specifications for the new product they ordered. Everybody was frustrated: Sales, because the customer kept changing the specifications (specs) – sometimes daily; Design because they could not get started on their work; both departments because they were frustrated with the customer (as well as the Prototyping department who was awaiting the design to start their work). Even the customer was frustrated because the Design department wasn't working on the product "redesign." Tension was high among the departments, with a great deal of finger-pointing. The problem was that the customer couldn't define their requirements, or they were unachievable. Design began creating the new product version, but the customer continued to change the specs, and several redesigns were necessary. This situation caused problems in all departments and disrupted the organizational process flow. The product was eventually shipped on time by sacrificing the schedule of other customers' orders and hiring additional staff on the weekends to expedite the shipping. The cost to the business (both dollars and morale) bit into the profit they made on the product and slowed the schedule of other products (increased labor costs, again, to ship and other frustrated customers). The irony of this case is that the CEO initially called me in to "fix" a senior leader who was suspected of being (but was not) the "problem." As process improvement guru Geary Rummler (1995) said, "If you pit a good performer against a bad system, the system will win almost every time." That is most certainly the case here.

LEADERSHIP WHACK-A-MOLE

Problem-solving techniques don't always examine a problem regarding the system or process it is in. Instead, they isolate the suspected causes of the problem, often without determining the effect any solution might have on the organization and, consequently, on the quality and effectiveness of the solution. Solution-generation techniques, such as brainstorming, often become a consensus method open to bias and undue influence of problem-solving team members. We can't deny that certain team members have more influence than others – executive and senior managers, certain departments, or individuals – and can sway the selection of a solution to the problem. When this type of internal political influence occurs, we are again faced with the dilemma of going along with the ill-fated solution or doing our best to refocus on a *realistic solution*. The process management method relies on measurement and data to decide how to locate and solve a problem. It minimizes the bias and influence of the solution selection. Different methods and resources assist in selecting the best solution and defining ideal actions.

One issue of note: making improvements in a process can incur a financial cost. This was a barrier to some when process improvement was formally introduced in the 1960s (although simple, intuitive forms have existed since prehistoric times, especially since the Industrial Revolution). Management mindset is too often set on saving or minimizing dollars spent on an "improvement." Any process improvement (e.g., hiring additional staff) may cost dollars. Still, we need to examine that in terms of overall cost-benefit, customer retention, and repeat purchasing. We sometimes look solely at the improvement costs rather than the benefits.

Process Management creates a collaborative, quality-focused, data-driven approach. We can see the organization as a "system" with interlocking "processes" within a functional design. Figure 5.2 shows an example of this.

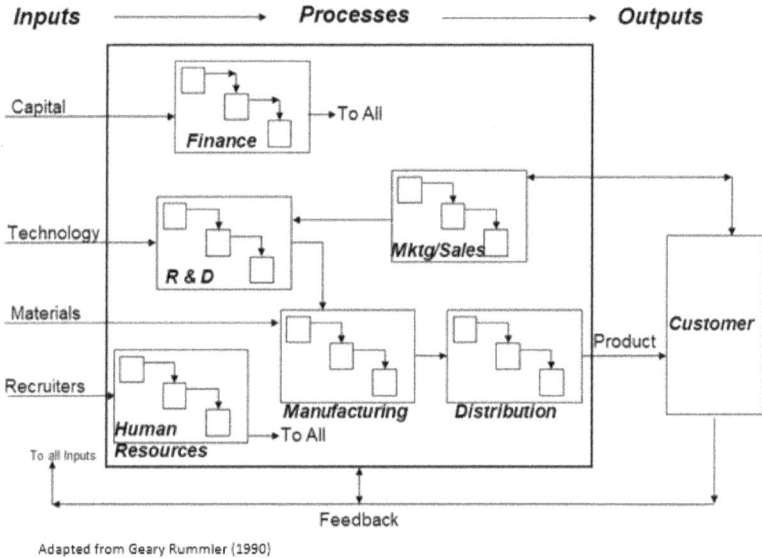

Figure 5.2. The business as a system

While Process Management is still used today, the method became widespread in the 1990s with the advent of Total Quality Management (TQM) in the United States. Many "quality improvement" programs have appeared and have been implemented by organizations of all sizes and purposes (private, public, nonprofit, and government). For most organizations, however, "TQM" became another "Flavor of the Month" (F.O.T.M.). Perhaps it was the cost of implementing a program or of maintaining it that caused its demise. Perhaps it was "we don't have the time or the staff load." Whatever the causes, TQM became an F.O.T.M.

Fortunately, TQM evolved into or was replaced by other methodologies that utilize process improvement and management. These include:

- Lean Manufacturing
- Lean Thinking
- Six Sigma
- Lean Six Sigma
- Agile Manufacturing
- Flow Production

While this book does not intend to go deeper into these methods, we should recognize that process management is used primarily in larger manufacturing companies (like Toyota, Intel, John Deere, and Nike) but can be effective in customer service.

RIC'S RESPONSE TO MEETING AND IMPROVING CUSTOMER SATISFACTION

I finish my perspectives on "customer service" by addressing the ongoing struggle most healthcare organizations and providers have faced over the past few decades – the challenge of creating a positive patient experience! I have spent most of my career in the healthcare industry, and ever since I can remember, the challenge of creating a positive patient experience has been "front and center!" Jeff introduced this chapter with his perceptions and questions about his recent inpatient hospital experience. I believe his perceptions and questions are not unique – millions of patients have had the same experiences and asked the same questions.

Senior leaders often make the mistake of jumping to conclusions about how to solve chronic problems with expensive and poorly thought-out solutions. A few years ago, I was asked to develop a "communications" training program for several hundred registered nurses who were periodically requested to assume supervisory responsibilities for their assigned departments. Both staff and patient complaints were being continually received within this organization. The senior nursing leader was convinced that the root cause of the problem was the lack of appropriate and compassionate interpersonal communication between the supervisory nurses, nursing staff, medical staff, patients, and patient's family. Upon further analysis and questioning, I learned that the supervisory nurses rotated through assignments once every 2 to 3 months, typically for no more than 2 to 3 sequential shifts. Most supervisory nurses were regular members of the department teams, and most treasured the "peer-to-peer" relationships they had with other members of their teams. There was no confirmed job description for the supervisor nurse role and no clear expectations for the ongoing appropriate communication. I ultimately recommended to the senior nursing leader that "permanent" supervisory nurses be assigned to each department and on each shift. I suggested updating the job description for the supervisory roles. This included clarifying the essential duties and requirements for each person in the role and the leadership skills needed (like communication). After the restructuring, the Organizational Development team gave specific training to the supervisor nurses and suggested individual development as needed. By taking a focused and precise approach, we saved time and money while holding ourselves accountable for changes in behavior and patient satisfaction, which led to successful clinical outcomes.

We'll talk about the significance of building and nurturing strong, high-performing cultures in an upcoming chapter. For now, we stress the importance of senior leadership and supporting mid-level leaders to continuously reinforce customer service decisions that occur as close to the primary customers as possible. This can only be achieved by selecting, developing, and strengthening the best talent with the right values and supporting behaviors on the front line of every enterprise.

We emphasized in the previous chapter, the importance of focusing on performance management and choosing the best talent to meet and exceed customer expectations. Also critical is that, through ongoing oversight and observation, we become keenly aware of individuals on our teams who promote dysfunction, conflict, and ultimately hostility among the other team members and, most importantly, with the customers and clients of our organizations. We define these individuals as "toxic," people who often creep into our organizations unexpectedly to make everyone around them just as miserable as they appear to be. In the next chapter, let's look at toxic people in the workplace.

LESSONS LEARNED

Identifying and Meeting Customer Needs

1. We must target the right customers by identifying their requirements and deciding whether we desire to -or can- serve them. Sometimes, we don't select certain customers because improving processes to meet their requirements does not make financial sense. We would be wasting our time collecting requirements from the wrong customers.

2. We need to view our relationships with customers as "partnerships" (not in the legal sense) to support each other's growth and continuous improvement strategies.

3. To meet customer requirements, we can use process management, which involves continuously analyzing and improving processes.

4. We must view the business as a "system" with interlocking key processes.

5. We must design our "customer satisfaction" programs around the idea that customer requirements will be met when we ensure that our internal functions meet their input and output requirements.

6. We must commit the resources (time, dollars, staff) to assuring the program's success. We can no longer rely on the crutch of "we don't have the time" to implement this.

Chapter 6

Dealing with Toxic People

When the Moles with Sharp Teeth Whack Back!

CHALLENGE QUESTIONS FOR THE READER:

1. As a leader, how do you deal with toxic employees and leaders in your business?
2. Do toxic people in your organization tend to get promoted or given more responsibility? Why do you think that is?
3. What is the effect of toxic workers on your organization or team performance?

RIC SHARES HIS EXPERIENCE WITH TOXIC PEOPLE

We have all worked with them – people who can undermine, sometimes very subtly, the best intentions and actions of our committed team members. They can be found at any level of an organization, and regardless of the formal authority these individuals may have, they can cause great harm to the cultural and emotional well-being of people and corporations. Here are the traits I have *observed* in what many of us have come to know as "toxic" people. They:

1. Take great pleasure in pointing out the mistakes and faults of others, particularly if the others have achieved success or have received positive recognition from senior-level leaders.

2. Rarely take responsibility for negative outcomes or mistakes and will only offer apologies if forced to do so by higher levels of authority.

3. Are generally withdrawn, preferring to exercise subtle sabotage behind the scenes while coming across as respectful, policy-abiding corporate citizens.

4. Are often "syrupy sweet" around authority, portraying an air of piety and self-righteous dignity while seizing every opportunity to denigrate the reputations or character of those they perceive to be threats.

5. Will often purposely withhold information to sabotage those whom they inwardly despise.

6. Generally resist positive change, recognizing that the proposed changes could undermine their current level of control and emotional security.

7. Will rarely take a stand or form an opinion that contradicts formal authority, always desiring to appear supportive of the direction senior leaders reinforced.

8. Will often take credit for or embellish their roles in organizational successes, even if they have little or nothing to do with the successes.

Toxic people are dangerous to us as individual leaders and to the organizations they purport to support. Toxic people often have very low levels of self-esteem. Most of us could fall prey to some of the behaviors of low self-esteem. If left unchecked, low levels of self-esteem can lead to toxicity in our behavior.

I share an example of one highly educated, intelligent, and extremely persuasive leader I worked with in the past. My first impression of them was very positive. However, over time, I kept hearing about decisions they would make or things they would say that were creating hostility that was counterproductive and drove some of our best people away. What was so challenging was how charming they were to those who did not work with them regularly. Complaints to senior leadership about them fell on deaf ears because they had an extremely positive perception of them. If a leader complained too loud or too often about these toxic people, they might be shown the door... and some were shown the door! In my interactions with them, I found them manipulative and untruthful about actions we agreed to or that could benefit the organization. They would often resort to manipulation when they felt the need to defend their turf or when they lacked expertise or knowledge on a particular subject. They frequently embellished their credentials and insignificant initiatives that they and their team had undertaken. They ultimately left the organization because of the isolation they created for themself – no one wanted to deal with them, and every effort was typically made to avoid them.

Bob Moawad, a close friend and mentor of mine, said that when we are no longer able to do what we have tied our self-worth to, we risk losing our self-identity. (personal discussion with Bob Moawad, 1984). Bob authored the curriculum known as *Increasing Human Effectiveness* (1979), which thousands of leaders have experienced over the past three decades. In that curriculum, Bob outlines some key steps for developing and reinforcing a healthy level of self-esteem:

1. Recognize that you are beautiful and unique just the way you are.
2. Get away from believing that you compete with others.
3. Recognize that self-worth is innate. Your actions and decisions do not determine your worth.

4. Accept 100% accountability for your actions and decisions.
5. Maintain a thought process that reinforces alignment with your values, avoids wishing harm on yourself or others, and reinforces a willingness to accept the consequences of your actions.
6. Recognize that mistakes are stepping stones to achievement.
7. Recognize that life is a journey to be embraced one day at a time.
8. Recognize that praise pays – even when things are not going well. Catch yourself and others in the act of doing things right.

When considering the people we have or currently work with, whom we may have or now consider toxic, it's crucial to remember that their actions are possibly a result of chronic low self-esteem. Some might say these individuals need a "little more love." And that may be true *outside* of the workplace. As business owners and leaders, we have a responsibility, first and foremost, to enable the successful operation and continuation of our various enterprises. Although we want to assist individuals with chronically low self-esteem and toxic behaviors, we have limitations in the support we can offer without compromising the well-being of our customers/clients and team members.

JEFF ANALYZES RIC'S EXPERIENCE WITH TOXIC PEOPLE

Ric is correct about the characteristics and impact of people we call "toxic" in the workplace. Manager and staff toxicity is not usually at the forefront of our organizational discussions, yet research and experience tell us it should be. Whether from the top of the hierarchy or a co-worker, toxicity creates consequences if not dealt with soon and firmly. Toxic workers cause their teammates (and managers) to be more stressed, less productive, and more easily burned out, with lower morale among team members and higher turnover, and there can be a negative impact on family life.

Often, toxic workers are not disciplined or corrected; instead, they get promoted. Why is this? In many organizations, workers or managers are promoted because they perform well – in spite of their toxic behavior (which sometimes is not even seen by management). Ric referred to this in his description of the persuasive leader he worked with who made themself look good while manipulating others. Senior leaders, he wrote, did nothing about the complaints they received about them. I think the toxic leader was either a good performer or politically astute to avoid the consequences of their behavior. Or perhaps the organization's entire culture was toxic and allowed them to behave this way.

Some experts on toxic culture believe that there are leaders who suffer from psychological issues that lead to toxic behavior. One personality that I have seen is the "narcissist." This toxicity shows itself as needing attention, grandiosity, and manipulating others. There are numerous causes for toxic behavior, and low self-esteem can be a contributing cause. It is solely my opinion that Ric's leader may have been compensating for a psychological deficit by exhibiting toxic behaviors or may have had a toxic personality. Narcissists are out for themselves and are not team players.

In some companies, toxicity is a part of the culture and starts at the top. When a CEO and senior leaders have a toxic mentality, it drives the rest of the organization to behave similarly. Workers look to senior leaders for direction about how to behave in the organization. When they see the people at the top behaving with toxic behavior, they feel a license to behave the same. When toxicity ingrains itself into the culture, it is difficult to eliminate. In these situations, we see an increase in the symptoms mentioned above, including employee turnover. How many people do you know who left their companies because of the toxic culture of the organization or of the team they are a part of? I know quite a few (myself included). Because the CEO drives the culture, toxic organizations need the commitment of the top leader to change it. However, one problem is that many CEOs don't know how to change their culture or behavior and require outside experts to guide or coach them. Although it is not within the scope of this book to delve into methods and interventions to change a toxic culture, I will say that the methods that hold promise are coaching the toxic actor, management discussions with staff, team discussions on norms, and setting clear expectations for behavior.

As Ric cited, complaints to management or Human Resources about toxic performers often go unaddressed. This may be because few people internally know how to deal with it – whether it's correcting the behavior of a peer or the company culture. So, the problems remain, and good people leave. For leaders to be terminated for complaining about a toxic senior leader tells me that the culture itself was toxic and reinforced by senior leaders, most likely the CEO. Sometimes, peers or subordinates retaliate against the toxic leader. The isolation the toxic leader experienced from others in Ric's description may have been a form of retaliation.

Toxicity in the workplace is a serious problem. When we think about the consequences of the problem, there is a cost to the company in terms of staff and manager attrition and decreased performance and productivity. Purushothaman and Stromberg (2022) estimate the cost of U.S. workplace toxicity at $50 billion annually. It's time to clean up this toxic mess. I share my own experience with workplace toxicity below.

My most potent experience with a toxic work environment came as a management consultant for a professional services company. My first years there were enjoyable. We had a fun and productive team that provided great client service. We lost some of our team members, and then our manager was replaced by a manager with a different style. Our first manager was highly engaged with the team. The new manager was not. We had new team members who created a clique. Our strong team vanished and was replaced with an "everyone for themselves" culture. One of our team members avoided conflict to the extent that they would walk out of meetings when confronted with a potential conflict. The manager excused their behavior by saying that they were "sensitive." Issues never got dealt with or resolved. Communication shut down, and team members stopped working with each other. Customers complained about their poor service and many long-term clients quit doing business with us. This exemplifies how leaders can create and maintain a toxic culture that impacts a business. This underscores the importance of leaders effectively navigating and managing conflict, a capability we will address in the next chapter. As leaders, most of us have worked with toxic people. The way we engage with them can determine whether we become victims of that toxicity or manage through that toxicity to support the organization's best interests. In the next chapter, we will address the topic of conflict management and how to effectively support successful resolutions.

LESSONS LEARNED

Dealing with Toxic People

1. There are 8 critical traits that characterize toxic people.
2. Psychological issues – especially low self-esteem- are key factors in toxicity.
3. Author Bob Moawad (*Increasing Human Effectiveness*) believes that healthy self-esteem can be developed.
4. Toxicity is not usually discussed in the workplace; complaints are usually not dealt with.
5. Toxicity impacts teammates. It creates stress, reduces productivity, promotes burnout, lowers morale, and increases turnover.
6. Toxicity can be a part of the culture – at the organization or team levels.
7. Toxicity costs American business $50 billion annually.

Chapter 7

Managing Conflict

When Different Agendas Provoke the Moles

CHALLENGE QUESTIONS FOR THE READER:

1. How does your organization generally deal with conflict? (e.g., confront it, avoid it, compromise?)
2. The workforce is getting more diverse in their values, purpose, gender, culture, language, etc. How has this affected conflict in your organization or team?
3. How effective and adaptable is your conflict "style" in dealing with conflicts?
4. How can conflict be healthy for a team?
5. Think of an example of how a change in your organization or team created a conflict.

In the famous line from the late Kenny Rogers' classic song "The Gambler," the choices we have about how to play our hands in a card game rings true for how, as leaders, we manage the many ways we manage conflict. Later in this chapter, we will discuss the natural "styles" that we are inclined to demonstrate when faced with unexpected conflict. No doubt some of you have experienced negative outcomes from conflicts you have been engaged in. In some cases, you may have even felt that your jobs were in jeopardy because of an ongoing or single significant conflict you may have experienced. One of the more energetic and outspoken executives we worked with during our careers said, "If you are doing your job and executing as expected, after 5 to 7 years in your job, you will have conflicts with enough people to put your position in jeopardy." They were so right!

Should we shy away from conflict? The answer is a resounding "No"! Conflict is inevitable. The key to effectively managing the conflict is to fully understand the root causes and, with the other parties in the conflict, work together to construct a mutually agreeable resolution (much easier said than done!) Three key factors drive our natural response to conflict: 1) our ability to comprehend the nature and causes of the conflict, 2) our personal values as they relate to the nature of the conflict and the issues involved, and 3) our subconscious, natural tendencies for engaging in conflict.

RIC'S CONFLICT STORY

I was told about a conflict involving a highly talented and strong-willed technical leader. Their extensive technical background in their area of specialization allowed them to successfully plan and execute cost-effective improvement projects. This leader relentlessly focused on doing what *they thought* was best for the organization, even when it meant disregarding the personal preferences and desires of other leaders. This leader often interacted with other organization members in an assertive manner but always maintained an appropriate level of tact. The leader's decision-making and interaction with those disagreeing leaders were allegedly seen as offensive and disrespectful. In summary, the organization's opposing leaders collaborated to fabricate a story of unethical practices by the technical leader. This ultimately led to the leader's involuntary termination from the organization. It was a textbook case of insecure leaders jeopardizing the reputation and career of a determined leader striving for the organization's benefit! It's not a healthy way to manage conflict.

Here are practical steps to effectively manage conflicts and maintain credibility while working with conflicting parties for the best resolution:

1. Take a deep breath, pause, and listen to the other party's and your own concerns.
2. Determine the urgency of the situation you are engaged in. Is it a serious or potentially catastrophic situation that could threaten others or the entire organization? If not, then with the agreement of the other parties, give yourselves some time to gather additional information, think and analyze the driving and restraining forces, and schedule a time to reconvene to generate alternatives for addressing the issue at hand. If it is a serious situation, take deep breaths and address the situation assertively with confidence and conviction. If you have a tendency to avoid conflict, you may need to take on a more assertive position. Others may not like your approach, but it may help to reduce the conflict.
3. Seek to fully understand the people in the conflict by understanding their motives, desires, and expected outcomes. Be willing to understand and question your own motives and desires.
4. The opposing parties should generate potential alternatives to resolve the conflict while considering the goals of the organization.
5. Identify other leaders and stakeholders within the organization who could consider the agreed-upon alternatives. With the input of the other parties, select and commit to alternative approaches for resolving the conflict.

LEADERSHIP WHACK-A-MOLE

A self-assessment and conflict styles instrument I have used successfully with many different groups and individuals is the Thomas-Kilmann Conflict Styles Inventory (1974). Through a process of self-discovery and team transparency, those I have worked with have addressed chronic and disabling conflicts existing within their organizations by examining their natural conflict tendencies and understanding the circumstances and forces creating the conflict. They then discover a collaborative approach to developing and implementing sound strategies for addressing the conflict in a way that benefits the enterprise. We rarely approach unexpected conflict in a collaborative mode, and that is why leaders need to know what their natural tendencies for dealing with conflict look like. The Thomas-Kilmann Inventory categorizes the natural conflict styles, or tendencies, into five different groups: Competing, Avoiding, Accommodating, Compromising, and Collaborating. If we are aware of what our natural conflict styles are, we can adjust our styles to respond appropriately to the situation. That's why the "deep breath" pause is so often the best initial approach to conflict. The pause gives us time to think through how to manage the conflict in the most productive way.

JEFF'S RESPONSE TO RIC'S CONFLICT STORY

In my experience, most people in the workplace are conflict-averse. Although sometimes an effective style, "Avoiding" can be detrimental to the welfare of the individual, the team, and the organization. I worked with a team member who created a great deal of conflict with me. As I was told, they applied for my position at the same time I did but did not get the job. Someone told me that the other person was disappointed not to have been chosen. They would often go over my (and my boss') head to talk to the Vice President of Operations to propose new programs without my knowledge. The Vice President told them to speak with me about the ideas each time, but they never did. As I implemented new programs, they did whatever they could to undermine the programs' success. Twice, they manipulated leadership into putting newly developed programs on hold. I had several discussions with this individual, trying to understand the root of the conflict. I used a Compromising style and then a Competing style. Neither worked. The Vice President was unwilling to intervene to manage the conflict or make a decision on the programs. This toxic person was working from jealousy about someone else getting the job. They were self-centered and thought more about themself than the business – and management let them get away with it.

It's amazing that with all the conflict management training we've provided employees and leaders over the decades, we're still not good at resolving conflicts. The causes of conflict avoidance are our lack of understanding of the nature and causes of the conflict, our personal values, and our natural tendencies for how we engage in conflict. Let's also consider the business culture and the team's subculture. For a manager to condone a team member for creating conflict (as described in the preceding paragraph), one can understand the culture of this organization – and it's not a productive one! Organizational cultures are no less susceptible to such behaviors and practices. We tend to behave like our leaders and how they expect us to act.

Patrick Lencioni, the author of *The Five Dysfunctions of a Team* (2002), believes that fear of conflict keeps teams from achieving commitment, accountability, and results (as well as damaging trust within the team). Lencioni argues that conflict can be managed in healthy and constructive ways to create a thriving team. While it can be managed, our fear of dealing with conflict also exists. I sat in on a staff meeting at a large manufacturing company where, in discussion, participants were expected to "challenge" each other. This challenge is a form of "controlled conflict." In most organizations, this would be ineffective. Except at this company, it was a constructive practice that promoted innovation, collaboration, and continuous improvement. So, as long as it is handled constructively, organizations can use conflict as a productive tool.

As we enter the new age of work, conflict prevention and resolution will become critical skills and mindsets. With the dissolution of the command-and-control leadership style, conflict suppression tactics like the one I mentioned above will be replaced with an earnest effort to utilize Ric's practical advice on managing conflict. We will likely see more conflict as networks and cross-functional project teams diversify. When Engineering, Accounting, Manufacturing, frontline workers, and Sales are all members of an ad-hoc problem-solving team, the potential for greater conflict is more likely than conflict self-contained in a functional team.

The transitioning workplace and jobs will create conflict that must be resolved for the business to grow and adapt to the changing environment and markets. To be innovative (a requirement for growth and survival), top management will decentralize power and decision-making to diversified, cross-organizational teams. This distribution of power and decision-making will generate even more conflict among team members and between the managers of those team members.

Expectations for conflict prevention and resolution must come from managers in terms of how they reinforce, manage, and coach their people. Extensive training will be required to ensure that all employees utilize conflict management skills. Managers must be trained in giving feedback, coaching, and reinforcing their teams in applying conflict management skills.

RIC DISCUSSES DEI INITIATIVES AND ORGANIZATIONAL CONFLICT

There has been much discussion around "DEI" over the last several years, particularly following the fatal George Floyd incident in Minneapolis in 2020. DEI, or "Diversity, Equity, and Inclusion," has evolved as a cultural, leadership, and employee awareness initiative designed to foster more inclusive, equitable relationships and outcomes in our businesses. While the intent is noble, the methods used to introduce and sustain formal DEI efforts have often caused conflict in participating organizations. Many self-ordained "diversity consultants" have introduced DEI initiatives in client organizations with varying levels of success. When the business owners are not involved in designing how DEI initiatives are introduced, we too often see disconnects between the consultants and the business stakeholders. The disconnects occur when the sponsoring business leaders and stakeholders cannot see or describe the link between the DEI initiative and the business priorities. The disconnects can lead to conflict among stakeholders in the organization, especially when there are conflicting priorities and expectations for DEI initiatives. From my experience as a past sponsor and participant in DEI initiatives, the best approach begins with creating an "inclusive" work culture - one that places a high priority on mutual respect, kindness, empathy, and compassion. It is a culture that reinforces the importance for all individuals associated with the business to be involved and included in transparent, honest, and safe interpersonal communication and relationships.

LEADERSHIP WHACK-A-MOLE

In the healthcare organization where I served as the Corporate Director of Learning & Organizational Development, I observed the successful launch of formal "DEI" initiatives where the primary focus was on "inclusion." This included setting clear expectations and reinforcing them through leader development and staff education, as well as the importance of treating each other and our guests with respect and dignity. The goal of those efforts has been to bring the people of the organization together, regardless of the unique backgrounds they are coming from and regardless of their individual preferences and traits. This focus on unity and collaboration is becoming a catalyst for a more compassionate, caring, and respectful work environment where all constituents of the organization – patients, visitors, medical staff, volunteers, and our employees – perceive a safe, non-threatening environment to receive, provide, and deliver quality care in. This effort has had the impact of minimizing inappropriate and unproductive conflict. Augmenting the DEI efforts will be a more robust, concentrated effort to train the leaders and caregivers to manage conflict constructively, emphasizing collaboration and joint problem-solving. We found that when our leaders, staff, and providers feel safe, supported, and included as respected, contributing members of their teams, their behavior positively impacts their interactions with the patients and visitors. This positive interaction, and ultimately higher patient experience scores, translates into higher levels of community support, higher patient volumes, enhanced employee engagement, and solid financial returns for the health system!

Conflict in organizations is inevitable, and we must learn to deal with it constructively. With the prospects of change forever on our horizon, we will focus on its nature and how we, as leaders, need to be ready to navigate the landscape of change.

LESSONS LEARNED

Managing Conflict

1. Each of us has a natural conflict style that we can adapt when needed. This gives us choice about how we manage conflict situations.
2. In addition to our individual styles, conflict management is influenced by the organization or team culture.
3. Conflict can be constructive – even healthy – to a team if facilitated well and supported by leadership (see Lencioni, 2002).
4. More conflict will appear as network and cross-functional project teams diversify their membership.
5. Decentralization of power and decision making in the organization will generate conflict among teams and managers.
6. Leaders must reinforce managers and hold them accountable to support and coach conflict prevention and resolution.
7. DEI (Diversity, Equity, and Inclusion) efforts in the workplace may expand opportunities for conflict as differing beliefs, values, cultures, and customs interact more frequently. Be aware of this dynamic.
8. All teams and individuals (including contingent workers) must be trained and proficient at conflict prevention and resolution.

***

Chapter 8

Navigating the Rapids of Change

Predicting the Moles' Next Positions

CHALLENGE QUESTIONS FOR THE READER:

1. In your experience leading a change initiative in your organization or with your team, what made it successful or unsuccessful?
2. In your leadership roles, what tools or resources would have been helpful to more effectively navigate the change? How has your organization's culture affected change initiatives?
3. To what degree do you think employees should participate in change initiatives?
4. What change model do you use when planning and implementing a change?

Too often, we hear the stories about and have witnessed the fallout from organizational change initiatives getting derailed, creating frustration for stakeholders and often causing leaders to lose their jobs. If this has happened to you or someone you know, some of what we cover in this chapter will sound familiar. What we hope to do is enable you to expect, analyze, avoid, and recover from failed change initiatives. More importantly, our goal is to offer guidelines and tools to enable you to plan for and successfully execute change initiatives. We recognize that every leader will face challenges in managing personal and organizational change, especially during market disruptions.

RIC'S CHANGE LEADERSHIP CHALLENGE

I remember hosting a dinner with some close friends one evening in our home. After dinner, while enjoying conversation, my friend asked our 7-year-old daughter what her daddy did for work (they knew full well what my job was but wanted to hear from my young daughter's perspective what I did for a living). In a sassy tone and with her hands on her hips, she stated, "My dad is in charge of meetings where he works, and he hates it!" That is what she had heard from me night after night when I came home from work, emotionally spent and spouting off about one challenging meeting after another. While her remark was humorous, I can now see how my daily transparency negatively impacted her perspective of "adult work." (Today, I am happy to see her positive attitude towards work, striving for excellence while also prioritizing a healthy work-life balance. She is now a respected, tenured university history professor, passionate about helping others expand their awareness. But she still doesn't like too many meetings!)

The truth was that I held a respected role as a senior HR executive at a prestigious metropolitan healthcare organization. I was given responsibility for leading a change effort to align our services with patient-centered care. It was a pleasure to lead and collaborate with other leaders and medical professionals to bring about the changes. It was a big endeavor but one worth undertaking. The board of directors, senior leaders, and most medical staff were on board with the desired outcomes for the changes. After a full year of analysis, multiple meetings, and extensive collaborative planning, we were ready to launch the change effort. Embedded in the plan was the need to reallocate several leaders to different roles and, sometimes, help those individuals find employment elsewhere. We didn't know much about reallocating people until we reached the final stages of the planning.

When certain members of our clinical leadership team learned of the planned reassignment of tenured clinical staff, an unanticipated resistance arose. The resistance grew to a boiling point, spilling into the ears of our senior Operations leaders. The resistance grew stronger and loud enough to halt the plan's implementation. Clinical leadership called for a "second opinion" from an external consulting group. Over the next several months, representatives from the consulting group found many opportunities to fault the original plan. They persuaded the senior leaders to pursue an alternative plan that was more in line with the changes *the consultants* wanted.

JEFF'S OPINION ABOUT RIC'S CHANGE LEADERSHIP CHALLENGE

Based on what Ric told me about this situation (I didn't experience it myself), this section is simply me forming opinions. These are not facts, just my opinion. Ric had asked for my "consultant" opinion of his situation. Here's what I told him:

There seemed to be little buy-in from clinical leadership in the pre-implementation stage. The information about reassigning or terminating clinical positions was surprising to them. The senior Operations leaders were on board with the plan until they got push-back from their clinical leaders. Since these decisions came at the end of the planning phase, it would have been best to push the implementation forward and work through the issues with those clinical leaders. However, that is not what happened.

As stakeholders plan and implement change initiatives, they should ask the following questions.

- *Do the key stakeholders understand and support the need for the change?*
- *What positive and negative consequences will occur during and after implementing the change(s)? And to whom?*
- *How extensively should the executive leaders and sponsors of the change involve the key stakeholders in the ongoing planning and the changes that might occur?*

In Ric's scenario, the senior Operations leaders must have held great power to redirect the plan to an outside consulting group. One wonders where the other plan proponents were, especially executive leadership. Why did they not express their thinking about this resistance? Were they involved in working with the Operations and clinical leaders to find a resolution? Were other options besides reassignment considered? Did they talk about it?

Executive leadership allowed the Operations leaders to seek a second opinion, even though the planning team had already agreed to the plan. There was a lack of leadership support and agreement that allowed a small group of clinical department leaders to exercise the power to scrap the project because of a handful of resistant lower-level leaders.

Again, the senior Operations leaders may have desired to eliminate the reassignments/terminations of the clinical leaders.

They ended up getting a "second opinion," in the long run, to scrap a change plan endorsed by senior and executive leaders; indeed, a plan that took a great deal of work over a year, involving a representative array of functional leaders. As the leader of this change process, Ric should have been the direct contact and partner with the outside consultants. They may have had little or no understanding of the organization's culture, the planning process, and the people involved in planning a major change. The senior Operations leaders oversaw the consultants' work and, as a result, they suggested a different approach. In the end, they did not implement the consultants' plan.

RIC'S FOLLOW-UP TO JEFF'S OPINION

I looked at the failed initiative again and considered Jeff's input. Then, I referred to my change management framework, called the IMPACT model, described below (Shriver, 2023). In hindsight, more attention could have been given to components P and C (below). The model asks pointed questions about the change. In collaboration with the right "stakeholders" involved in and supporting the change, it can be summarized as:

I–Information–what data, insights, and feedback do we need to support the change?

M -Magnitude–just how significant is this change compared to other organizational priorities? How much effort and attention does this change warrant? Should we delay prioritizing the change?

P-People – Who are involved in this change? Who are the sponsors, change agents, champions, recipients, customers, and other stakeholders?

A–Actions – What critical steps/actions must occur for the change to be implemented successfully, i.e., what is the project plan? What core processes are being driven by or impacting these people involved? How will potential process design occur, and by whom? How does the change get positioned among other organizational changes being managed?

C–Consequences, Communication – If the change is not successfully implemented, what will be the consequences to the people, organization, and customers? Alternatively, what are the rewards we will expect for successful navigation? Did we include the consequences and rewards in our project plan, with a special focus on the target audience(s) for communication?

T – Timing – Built into our project plan, when should key actions and critical communication occur to support the successful navigation of the change?

MORE FROM JEFF ON CHANGE

Ric's example of a failed attempt is typical of many organizational change programs -many of them fail. This section will explore some reasons for this and models for successful change.

One reason cited for people's resistance to change is their belief that they have something to lose. In Ric's hospital example, the change made the clinical leaders feel like they had something at stake - their positions or jobs. Could they have executed the change process differently? Of course. Perhaps the initiative might have been successful if the planning team used the IMPACT model.

LEADERSHIP WHACK-A-MOLE

I have observed that the lack of adequate planning is evident in many change management situations. Leaders do not always understand the change process and cannot make the changes they hope for. A failed program can devastate an enterprise, especially if the organization is in a fast-changing environment and cannot afford to keep the status quo. Many successful change initiatives I have seen or learned about are in large businesses and take years to complete. I have worked with scores of small and mid-sized companies that make significant organizational changes without a plan and often fail to achieve their desired outcomes. The consequences of a failed change initiative can be costly: employee resignations, decreased morale and motivation, reduced productivity, increased conflict among individuals and groups, loss of trust in management and leadership, and customer defections.

Ric's "change leadership challenge" was just that, a leadership issue. The committed support of top leadership is essential for successfully implementing any organizational change. In his example, senior leaders initially showed commitment. Still, they ultimately gave in to a small group that believed their interests were at risk instead of following a systematic change management process that could have resolved the problem.

A word on outside change management consultants. It is not unusual for a consultant or consulting group to not understand the planning that had gone on in the past, the culture and political dynamics of the organization, or the leaders and their interests in the change. The consulting group made little effort to understand which "players" should be included in the analysis of the change plan. If you choose to have a "change management" expert or group assist you in a change endeavor, be sure they become deeply "embedded" in the organization and serve as guides and facilitators to others.

They must understand your organization and its dynamics and people. Having a change method without understanding your business and its culture is insufficient. Those most knowledgeable about the change effort were not involved as an internal resource or in developing the new program (a genuine loss of knowledge, insight, experience, and information). The organization failed to implement the new change plan, and the desired outcome was not achieved.

JEFF'S BRIEF HISTORY OF CHANGE MANAGEMENT MODELS

I taught graduate-level Organization Development courses for twelve years. During that time, I conducted much research on the topic of change. Early change studies conducted in the 1980s and 1990s by American academics were often theoretical or anecdotal. However, some studies were empirical (Kanter (1983), Schaffer (1988), Kilmann (1988), D'Aveni (1989), Beer et al. (1990), and Kanter et al. (1992) and accurately described successful change processes in large businesses, such as General Electric, General Motors, Hewlett Packard, Apple, Delta Airlines, Motorola, IBM, Exxon, Chase Manhattan Bank, Allied Signal, and Northern Telecom. While these studies are not new, I have found a great deal of wisdom in their research results. From these studies, I identified trends in successful organizational change.

1. *External pressures* related to survival, competition, and profitability influenced organizations more when it came to making changes.

LEADERSHIP WHACK-A-MOLE

2. Change requires a *quick adaptation to the changing environment*. Subsequently, the organization needs *fast access to adaptive strategies*.

3. *Change is often driven by line - not top - management* and focuses on critical business needs and operational problems.

4. Change more often occurs at the *organization's periphery through local action* and then *spreads to the core* through top management support and vision (not mandate).

5. Innovative personnel (primarily managers) often create *adaptive solutions* to environmental change without the support or knowledge of top management.

6. *Change is a political process*; the solution is often selected based on its power base.

7. At the decentralized local level, *each business unit replicates* successful adaptive solutions, enabling them to implement the change at their own speed and in their own way.

8. Change occurs through *ad hoc arrangements*, not organizational system and structure change.

9. Implementing the change *aligns the systems and structure*.

10. Success is often circumstantial or a *matter of luck*.

11. *Cross-functional communication* is essential for developing adaptive solutions.

12. Top management *vision is critical* to successful change.

13. ***Experimentation and muddling through*** are necessary processes.

14. Replicating best practices from other organizations ***rarely assures success***.

15. Relevant ***behavior changes*** lead to culture change.

16. We must empower change agents with the ***freedom to innovate*** with resources, information, and support.

LATER STUDIES

In later studies, researchers such as Collins and Porras (1994), Kotter (1992,1995), Price Waterhouse (1995), Fitz-Enz (1997), Johnson (1997), Brown and Eisenhardt (1997), Robinson and Stern (1998), researchers found many of the same elements as the earlier studies. The Collins and Porras study, which examined 38 organizations over six years, is highly significant. Some of the visionary companies included 3M, American Express, Boeing, Citicorp, Ford, General Electric, Johnson & Johnson, Marriott, Merck, Nordstrom, Procter & Gamble, Sony, Wal-Mart, and Walt Disney.

Collins and Porras found successful companies were built upon an ideology of strong core values and a fixed sense of purpose. The strong culture fostered by this core ideology enabled the organization to innovate with new products and strategies. The organization's goals, strategies, tactics, and design aligned with the core ideology. These organizations were both dedicated to their culture and open to change, motivated by their desire to improve and willingness to try new things. Top management vision played a critical role in the success of the companies.

In my 1999 paper, *"How Organizations* Really *Change: A Research Model,"* I sketched a change model that incorporates key elements from these research studies (see Figure 8.1).

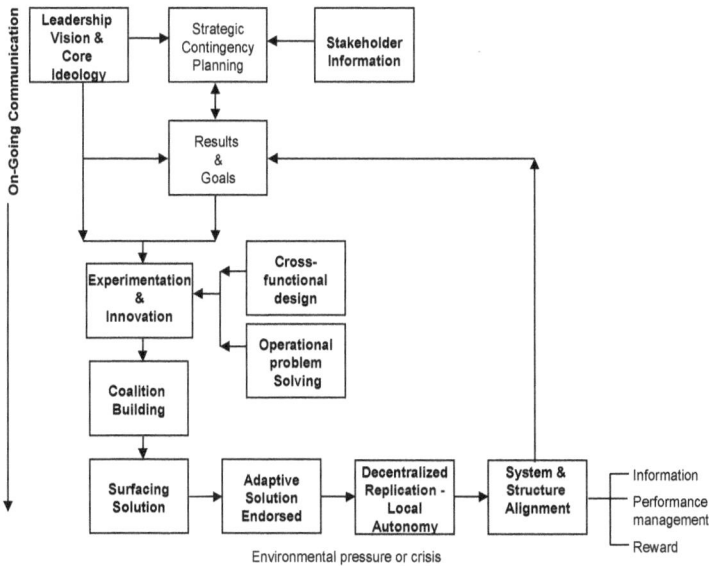

Figure 8.1. A Research-Based Model of Organizational Change

Here is a description of each step in the model:

On-Going Communication: Research shows that employees accepted a change when they understood the need for it. In these companies, top management ensured that all employees received ongoing information about the company's status in the marketplace.

When the environment worsened, associates understood the "bad news" and were willing to support - not resist - change.

Leadership Vision/Core Ideology: The companies studied had a vision of a future state from top management. This vision served several purposes that helped employees to accept change: 1) it held out a promise for tomorrow, 2) it provided a direction for the organization to take, 3) it created motivation for employees, and 4) it showed that change was not a "shoot from the hip" action but a logical step toward the vision. The core ideology (values and purpose) established a stable foundation from which the organization could stimulate progress through experimentation and innovation.

Strategic Contingency Planning: Successful organizations maintain a strategic view, scanning the environment for changes and assessing the feasibility of their projected results and goals. The organizations prepared for unexpected changes by adjusting their plans, objectives, resources, and outcomes.

Stakeholder Information: Many organizations sought broad-based stakeholder input to their environmental scanning for strategy and goal setting. ·

Results and Goals: Most companies drove change around the strategic results they intended to achieve. Change programs were not arbitrarily incorporated. They were chosen to achieve specific company results, not just to follow "Flavor of the Month" fads. Change agents were asked to achieve these results, not merely to implement a change for the sake of trying something different. The results guided innovation and experimentation. The goals set to achieve the results were challenging ones.

Driving Change with Vision & Results: Successful change management begins with vision and anticipated results. Top management communicates and inculcates a shared vision within the company. Most times, top management initiated change by communicating the expected results - without a mandate on how to achieve the results. Consequently, upper management refrained from loading "programs" top-down. Instead, organizational units could "experiment" with practical approaches to achieving the results.

Innovation: Line operating units used cross-functional communication to achieve desired outcomes. Top management first determines and communicates the results it wishes to achieve, then delegates and supports local, autonomous innovations to achieve those results. Top management does not impose large-scale, organization-wide change programs top-down. Instead, organizational units can "muddle" through "experiments" to achieve the identified results. This process happens swiftly, and the company channels its energy into this "innovative" change effort. The responsibility of developing the innovation is sometimes given to a single unit or team - it is not assigned to the entire organization.

Cross-Functional Design: In many research studies, successful organizations used a cross-functional organizational design to stimulate communication and innovation. In the early studies, the design was matrix management. In the contemporary studies, the design was project- and team-based.

Operational Problem Solving: Some studies showed that change comes from ad hoc arrangements in solving critical operational problems. In these situations, line management drives innovation by assembling ad hoc teams to solve a business problem quickly. These solutions can then be replicated in other parts of the organization.

Coalition Building: Changes created to meet the strategic results were often resisted. Despite opposition, the change agents collaborated with other "political" groups and wielded their influence to bring about the changes. Coalition building was also used to procure needed resources from across the organization to implement the change. Cross-functional organizational designs facilitated coalition building.

Surfacing Solutions: Company leaders who possessed political acumen and networking skills executed the plans. Timing was a critical factor in whether an innovation was accepted by top management. Innovators built coalitions to support the seeding and growth of the new idea and developed an alliance of supporters. Eventually, the innovators enlisted a top-management champion and surfaced the idea for implementation after building a critical mass of support. Once surfaced, the solution gained endorsement from top management for replication within the organization. Whether an endorsement will happen depends on whether an external environmental change is occurring or going to occur. At these times, top management saw the need for a new way of responding to change.

Decentralized Replication: As a team develops and shows success with a "piloted" model, other company units actively replicate the innovation process. Units can adapt the successful "model" to suit their needs and develop their own solution. Business units made changes that contributed to the organization's results rather than simply implementing a successful model in another business unit. This was often a process of "reinventing the wheel" with the benefit of continual "experimentation" and improvement.

System & Structure Alignment: Companies that successfully managed change revised their organizational structure and system *after implementation of the change*. Some conventional organizational change theories suggest that system and structure change should occur before or during implementation. However, studies show that the change process moves faster and can be more flexible to modification by waiting on structure and system change. Critical systems that require change are information, reward, and performance management systems. Aligning these systems with the change is necessary to support the right communication and behavior.

JEFF LOOKS AT CONTEMPORARY STUDIES AND MODELS

Contemporary studies incorporate essential elements of the earlier change models. Researchers developed these models nearly 30 to 35 years ago when the environment and markets were more stable than they are today, and organizational structures were more inflexible and "bureaucratic." Today's enterprises have become (out of necessity) more flexible with less complexity in their structure. Dynamic change is forcing many businesses to adjust to the way they operate as well. Newer change models can instruct us on how to make needed changes.

Earlier models presented change as a lengthy process. Many of today's models show change as an incremental, shorter, and ongoing process that can respond to faster changes. In the 1980s and 1990s, I remember the "debate" about how long a large-scale transformation takes. "Experts" predicted 3 to 5 years. Because of a more stable environment and markets, larger businesses had the luxury of taking years to transform, but not today. I remember when I worked with strategic planning horizons that were 5 to 10 years out. Now, many companies can't plan for more than a year out because of the fast-changing nature of their environment. When changes happen, companies need to make adjustments to their plans in the short term (sometimes for six months) for strategies, objectives, and resources. The best example I have seen in the past several years was the COVID-19 epidemic, which forced many structural and operational changes to organizations, some of which have become permanent (for example, hybrid and remote work). A rule of thumb has been that the larger the organization, the longer the timeframe for a change, but with incrementalism in planning and executing strategies, this is not necessarily the case today.

Academics and practitioners pondered the other question: should they make an organizational change on a large scale or in smaller increments? Studies have looked at this question, and "it depends." It depends on many considerations, including how quickly the change needs to be made. Does the change need to be "top-down" or "participative?" Are resources available to make the change? Is the organization's structure capable of handling the change? Can we adapt the current strategic plan to the change? Will the culture support successful change? Deciding on a change method requires an assessment of these conditions.

An organization cannot accomplish change with a one-size-fits-all approach. The consideration of many variables is daunting. There is no fixed timeline for a change to succeed. We see change management as a one-time thing instead of a continuous part of the organization's life. Change is always present and forcing us to adapt.

LEADERSHIP WHACK-A-MOLE

I have witnessed large-scale change efforts fail because too many additional external changes have occurred while implementing the original large-scale plan. No industry can escape change, although some industries are forced to change more slowly because of fewer environmental disruptions.

The trend in organizational change is to adopt a faster and incremental approach because of the rapid speed of change. James Brian Quinn's model of Logical Incrementalism (1980) (initially used for strategic planning) suggests that strategic decisions should be made in small, logical steps with flexible short-term goals. In this way, a business can manage itself by making decisional "pivots" when necessary. Other models view change management as a series of rapid "experiments" that can build on themselves and provide quick learning. Some models suggest creating a large-scale change plan and breaking it down into incremental segments, believing that as we build each step, we will eventually complete the entire plan or make changes "on the fly" without fully committing to all of the steps of the original longer-term plan.

Often, top leaders are inexperienced in the implications of the changes that prompt the need for effective management. Some leaders are naïve enough to believe that what they did that worked in the past will work again in the present. Other leaders have "pet" change ideas ("shiny new objects"), perhaps discovered at a conference or from a leadership book they read. Forcing a personal project on the entire organization is a bad idea unless the leader chooses an idea that aligns with the business needs and strategies and is willing to go through a "learning" process with others in the organization. Without a thorough assessment of the change and the organization's capabilities to make and manage the change, success is unlikely. Top leaders are not likely to know about things at lower levels that can impede a transformation effort, like poor worker morale and motivation, lack of trust in leadership, limited worker skills and capabilities, beliefs and habits that will interfere, limited resource availability, etc. We must do a great deal of front-end work to determine how to execute a change. Some leaders just don't do the work to ensure success. Perhaps that explains why so many change programs fail.

JEFF TOUCHES ON THE ROLE OF CULTURE IN TRANSFORMATIONAL CHANGE

In Chapter 9, we talk in greater detail about organizational culture. For our purposes here, let's look at culture as a factor in the change process. Many models and theories exist regarding workplace culture. From research and personal experience, we know that culture can "make or break" a change initiative. Using Edgar Schein's model (2019), the foundation of culture in an organization is the "beliefs" and "values" that most workers and leaders subscribe to (whether they are aware or unaware). Successful change programs rely on understanding the beliefs and values that shape behavior, as behavior change is critical. Changing beliefs requires complicated methods to enact. Think of beliefs in your organization. You may believe that "we are great because of how we've always done things" or "stick to the policies and procedures, and everything will run smoothly." These beliefs can impede change management programs and even derail them. To successfully implement a change program, it's important to understand the beliefs and values of the organization's culture. Changing culture requires everyone's commitment to altering beliefs and behaviors. Organizational change programs are no longer only "technical." We must engage the "human" side as well.

JEFF TALKS ABOUT DEALING WITH RESISTANCE TO CHANGE

People often resist change. There are many reasons for this. We frequently overlook these reasons and fail to incorporate them into the change plan. This leads to consequences, including poor morale, frustration, anxiety, fear, anger, decreased productivity, attrition, and lessened trust in leaders about knowing what they're doing. We need to attend to the human side of change. If not, we should expect resistance and failure. Resistance results from a cognitive dissonance between deeply ingrained beliefs and beliefs of a different way of doing things or a change in values (for example, "We are a product-driven company, not a customer-driven one.")

Worker participation in the change process can minimize resistance. However, participation means the change process may take longer than a top-down directive. When there is little time for a participatory approach, and change agents must make the change quickly, effective communication to employees and leaders explaining this is critical. I developed a change management program for a division of a large engineering company. In the opening executive session, I emphasized employees are more open to change when they know where the company stands in the market (based on a research study). The Vice President confronted me in front of the senior leadership team and said it was inappropriate to share that "kind" of information with workers. It would have been a great opportunity for a team discussion, but the Vice President just shut it down. (How's that for shaping culture?).

This experience with the Vice President helped me to understand that successful change must be driven by the company

CEO and senior leaders. Not only do they need to communicate the proposed change and the need for it, but they must also "walk the talk." They must model the behaviors and attitudes they will require from others. We must inform, train, and reinforce senior leaders to demonstrate these behaviors. How top leaders behave themselves will impact the success of the program. Too many CEOs delegate their pet "change" projects to lower-level managers who have limited understanding, information, skills, and resources to implement the project. In the meantime, a CEO attends a "CEO networking group" and comes upon a new idea for a project (and a consultant to implement it). Lower levels of the organization are left with the original change project hanging as a CEO implements another new pet project. And we wonder why so many transformation initiatives fail.

In the next chapter, we will focus on the notion that most businesses compete in rapidly changing environments, which require leaders to reinforce adaptability from a holistic open systems perspective. Such a perspective will enable leaders to respond to the changing demands, expectations, and requirements of their customers more precisely and effectively.

LESSONS LEARNED

Navigating The Rapids of Change

1. Organizational change is a political process.
2. Change agents need political, negotiating, and collaborating skills.
3. A model like IMPACT can assure a more effective change plan and implementation.
4. Changes done incrementally can be more effective than large-scale "top-down" programs.
5. Culture can "make or break" a change initiative.
6. All levels of leadership need to support the change initiative and buy into the methodology and key assumptions behind the planned change.
7. While it may take longer, employee participation in the change process reduces resistance to the change.

✱✱✱

Chapter 9

Open Systems

How One Mole Can Stir Up the Pack

CHALLENGE QUESTIONS FOR THE READER:

1. Why do you think it is that, after implementing a practice or program that "experts" have deemed as the best in class, other parts of your organization react negatively, don't accept and support, or create unexpected dysfunction? What has been your response when these kinds of reactions occur?
2. As a leader in your business, how can you influence other parts of the organization to support your change decisions and actions?
3. How does open systems thinking affect your business' ability to change and adapt?
4. What are some examples of unexpected outcomes occurring within your business as a result of a decision you made?

An open system is one that interacts and exchanges materials or information with its external environment. This exchange will be explained in greater detail later in this chapter. For our purposes now, consider the "systems" aspect, where each section of the organization is part of the whole (known as "holistic") that interacts with each other and the whole organization. A change in one part of the system will affect the whole system.

LEADERSHIP WHACK-A-MOLE

RIC'S EXPERIENCE WITH OPEN SYSTEMS

No doubt many of you have fallen prey to the F.O.T.M. (Flavor of The Month) phenomenon Jeff describes in his introductory remarks. A member of senior leadership or an external speaker prompts the launching of a new technology, process, or initiative. These tasks are often initiated because someone learned that they had worked somewhere else with purported positive results. These ideas and initiatives may not take into account the necessary infrastructure, the potential impact on other parts of the organization, and a proper assessment of their measurable impact on key performance indicators. We refer to these new ideas and initiatives as "*shiny new objects*" because they so often distract the focus of the entire leadership team.

One of the key things I had to learn as a Radioman during my enlistment in the Navy was how to appropriately "tune" radio transmitters to maximize the signal strength for our target destinations. Tuning required knowledge of atmospheric conditions, desired frequency, communication mode, and antenna length. Maximizing signal strength rarely involved maximizing transmitter power. Typically, the power amplification had to be moderated to produce the best and strongest signal.

The same radio transmitter principle can apply to the organizations we are trying to strategically manage. Our environments are always changing because of factors like market conditions, people, tools, technology, resources, and new revenue streams. Unless we are astutely aware of the changes occurring with the variables that affect our organizations, we can easily fall into the trap of assuming we must maximize the "power" we are investing in certain departments. Many times, we have the mindset that "more of the same" is the solution, especially when we come across examples of others using extra "power" (or extra resources) to yield positive results. That trap can easily apply to new ideas, concepts, programs, and initiatives that appear to be wonderful and may have worked well in certain environments and under certain circumstances. But, assuming that more of whatever the "*shiny new object*" is, the actions that claim to improve the organization's performance will often have the *opposite* effect. A good case in point follows.

An external consultant who I worked with a few years ago shared a story with me about a large consumer services organization that was being challenged with declining customer service ratings. In the consultant's work with the team leading the customer service improvement initiatives, they statistically showed that up to the point of marginal returns, staffing and productivity ratios had a direct correlation with customer service scores (i.e., if staffing for each unit was below acceptable levels, then customer service scores were also going to be below as well). Conversely, if staffing ratios were at an "acceptable" level, customer service scores could see an increase. Senior management didn't accept that staffing levels and customer satisfaction were correlated and told my consultant friend that staffing levels had nothing to do with high customer service ratings. In the end, the company teamed up with a different customer service consulting firm they had been exposed to at a recent national conference (*a shiny new object?*). The new consulting firm stressed the importance of regular training events for leaders where core customer service concepts were regularly and consistently downloaded for hopeful dissemination to geographically dispersed unit teams. In this case, senior leadership did not take a *systems* view of the problem. They simply assumed that staffing levels could not affect customer service ratings. Had they taken a more "*open systems*" approach, leadership might have analyzed the *whole system* – especially the feedback from the data – to more precisely recognize the offered solution. Like the pilot flying to Cali, the leaders were blinded by a preconception and disregarded the facts.

My friend assured me that over a few years, the company spent millions of dollars with no measured improvement in customer service ratings. The problem with this customer service intervention was that in open systems thinking, the program did not take into consideration all of the variables affecting customer service scores – an expensive and unsuccessful preconception. This program turned out to be a failed "Flavor of the Month" initiated by a "*shiny new object*" and myopic and fearful (of having to add additional staff) barriers to looking at other solutions.

As I assess the customer service challenges and leadership actions to remedy them, I am reminded of how critical it is that senior leaders possess critical, systems-thinking, and above-average cognitive skills. These capabilities are necessary to understand and respond to the environments with open systems thinking. If leaders understand the real challenges and changing markets they operate in, they can find innovative adaptive solutions. Unfortunately, I have witnessed "linear" (breaking down complex problems into smaller, manageable parts and analyzing each part individually) thinking in many of the organizations I have worked with. This contrasts with open systems thinking, which looks at the "whole" and how the parts fit together and interact with each other. Too often, organizations fail to fully recognize and take into consideration the factors within and outside of the organization that influence the business when shaping potential interventions or solutions.

In his book *Transforming the Future of Healthcare* (2024), Jason Wolf, Ph.D., (Author and President of the Beryl Institute), emphasizes that "to effectively succeed, we need to manage the points of interaction and the system around them. This commitment to broader considerations, to true systems thinking, becomes essential in our ability to better understand all the factors impacting the global health system, the practices engaged in locally, and the opportunities that healthcare has overall for constant improvement." Open systems thinking and practice can have a wide-ranging impact on business practices.

JEFF TALKS ABOUT OPEN SYSTEMS AND SOME IMPLICATIONS

I worked at a large organization in a changing industry that was once stable. Every year, the organization developed or updated a strategic plan and communicated the *intent* of the plan to divisions and departments. As department heads, we were then required to create a local "strategic" plan based on the company's plan (although we never saw the company plan itself). Not knowing the specifics, rationale, strategies, or goals of the company plan, we danced around with the information we had to create a departmental plan. Since we did not receive information on how the company's strategic plan addressed external or internal conditions, we did not take them into account when creating our plan. This, of course, is a "kiss of death" for a strategic plan. As the plan year progressed, we, at the department level, found it difficult to know if we were achieving any of the company's milestones because they were not shared with us. Instead, much of the work we did in the plan was reactive to the whims of senior leadership. We carried out our regular and ongoing work within our job functions and were occasionally requested by senior leadership to run a new project that may or may not have had any relation to the company's strategic plan. A *"shiny new object" is* at play. *Whack!*

The external environment experienced a quick and radical change that the company was unprepared for. The company lost about a third of its annual revenue and resorted to massive layoffs and operational selloffs to offset the revenue loss. One essential element of strategic planning is to expect a change that *may* occur and create a "contingency" plan in case it does occur. Despite engaging in "strategic" planning, the company failed to adequately prepare for the significant changes that did come, let alone how to capitalize on them. A rumor floated around that, despite having a strategic plan with sound input, the senior leaders felt they knew best how to handle the changes, as they had already grown the company to great profitability (remember the Flight 965 pilot?) By not following its strategic plan when the external environment radically changed, the company lost a significant amount of its revenue in a short time. So, as a part of a massive downsizing, I was out on my ass! *Whack!*

An example of an "open system" is strategic planning/strategic management. In Chapter 5, we used an organization map to illustrate the concept of open systems (Figure 5.2). This map shows how a business takes inputs, transforms them, and produces outputs with feedback. The essence of an open system is that it interacts with its environment and adapts in response to it. Figure 9.1 on the next page diagrams an open system.

Environment

Inputs→ Throughputs →Output

Boundary

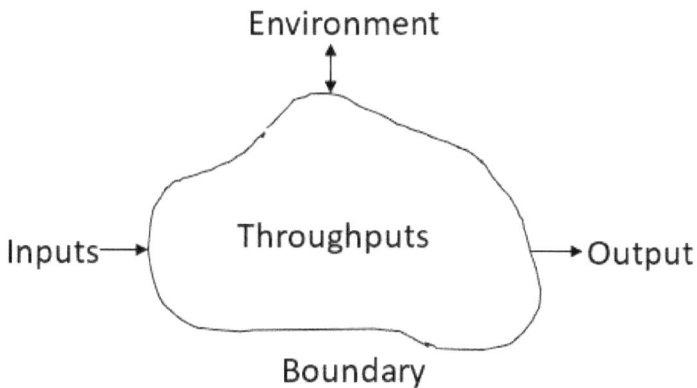

Figure 9.1 Simple Diagram of an Open System

The concept of an open system was originally developed in the natural sciences. A simple example of an open system is a flower. With defined boundaries, the flower takes in sunlight, water, and oxygen in a soil base (inputs) and transforms them into nutrients (processes and throughput), expelling carbon dioxide, seeds, and pollen (outputs). This dynamic employs processes to achieve survival and renewal. Without the "system" working as expected, the flower devolves into "entropy" and dies.

Figure 9.2 demonstrates the application of the open systems concept to organizations. Here, the organization, like the flower, receives input. These may be materials, people, technology, information, strategies, etc. These inputs go through processes in the transformation stage to become goods and services (output) that go to the market and customers. The organizational system has a defined, rectangular boundary, while the biological system has flexible and less defined boundaries because of natural evolution and change. The flower-as-system works naturally. There is no organization chart to "manage" the flower. Inputs are organic rather than "selected" in the flower "system." Transformation processes are also natural, not human-made. Nature – not people - designs flowers (although we are getting there with our methods of creating hybrids out of natural organisms and cloning).

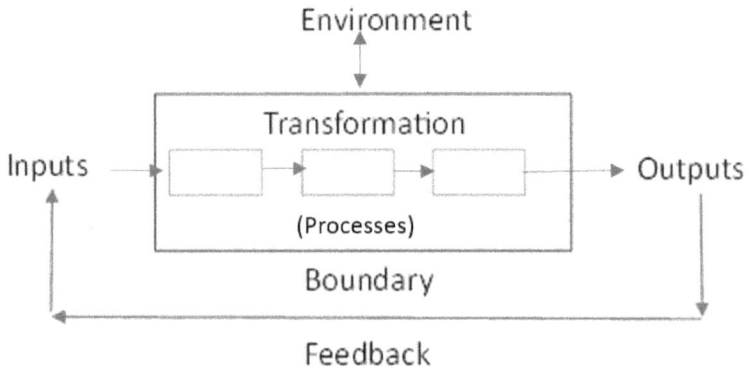

Figure 9.2. An Organizational System

Organizational systems have added a ***feedback loop*** to ensure that inputs and transformation work as designed. This is also a part of the control function. Natural organisms (like flowers and clouds) do not have a feedback mechanism. If the conditions are right, the flower grows, but it cannot "measure" the oxygen or water input to tell itself to "get back on track or improve;" it simply dies.

Researchers and philosophers speculate that the business organizational system surpassed its function of simply describing the way the system works to employing it as a control mechanism to provide profitable outputs to the market. With the Industrial Age, organizations redesigned such systems to better accommodate new forms of work - specifically, the assembly line and piecework. Throughout the 20th century, due to ongoing changes in the external environment, systems, and processes became more complex and more rigid in the formation of boundaries. While new products like TVs, cars, and home appliances gained popularity, the production and management systems remained mostly unchanged. The boundaries were still rigid, and processes were linear. And that's where we are today.

Throughout much of the 20th century, the environment and markets were relatively stable. Even during war times, organizational systems and structure remained the same (albeit speeded up). After World War II, technology and innovation exploded. In 1947, the invention of the transistor set the stage for the Information and Digital Ages. With this introduction, markets and the external environment began fluctuating. The eventual entropy (or at least revenue and profit declines) threatened the stability of the organizational system. Traditional companies are making internal changes today, such as staff cuts or "re-engineering," to adapt to changing markets and environments. That's the key–adapting to changes! As you can tell from your own experiences in the world of organizations, we don't always seem to know what to do–how to adapt to the proliferation of changes. So, we've continued doing what we always did–move the boxes around on the organization chart (or, as they say, rearrange the chairs on the Titanic)

Then came global competition. Before that, the United States produced most of the modern products consumed around the world. Then came people like Joseph Juran and W. Edwards Deming (Americans), who showed a crippled post-World War II Japanese economy how to produce goods–particularly electronics and automobiles - with greater quality and lower cost using "quality" methods like statistical process control (SPC). Soon, American pants were on fire. We were losing market share in industries such as electronics and automobiles. The environment changed, and global competition increased market choices for consumers. The whole rigid American organizational system went bonkers, trying to understand what went wrong. Some companies are still trying to figure it out. ***Whack!***

So, what did American companies do? They started borrowing technologies from the Japanese, particularly in auto manufacturing and other high-tech industries. For a ***handful*** of American companies, the introduction of "quality" technologies (generally called Total Quality Management in this country) has worked well. Most companies who tried it failed (I know. I was a part of two of them). Why? Those companies faced challenges in introducing new methods because of their inflexible systems and cultures, as well as lack of support from top leadership. The quality improvement interventions did not take a holistic analysis of the wide range of variables involved in improving quality within the enterprise. Where are we now?

We are trying like crazy to find answers to our internal and external problems. That explains why we spend $340 billion (Bersin, 2023) on training alone–not including other interventions and non-training programs. We're looking for the answer to the question of how we adapt to the tumultuous external and internal changes. Now, besides global changes, we see a major shift in customers' insistence on meeting their expectations for cost, quality, and schedule. Satisfying the customer has become a significant part of organizational strategy and practice. We are trying countless Flavor of the Month programs that have little or no effect on the company's performance. And don't forget the Millennials who are looking to run your company or department as soon as the new employee orientation concludes. Oh, yeah! I almost forgot about remote and hybrid working. And the inflationary cost of capital. Did I miss anything? Has the world gone crazy? No, it's just "man-made" evolution. We have replicated Newton's linear, mechanical world into organizational parts (like a clock). Too often, we fail to look at the whole system. Remember, in a system, every part affects other parts and the whole, so we must look at the whole. Oh gee, I almost forgot COVID-19. How was that for an organizational disruptor? It may have been the greatest blessing for business because it forced us to redesign our businesses and the nature of work and jobs. What's the next disruptor we don't know about?

We know from Open Systems Theory that when we change one part of a system, it affects the other parts and the whole. We use the term "suboptimize" to explain how one part of the system that optimizes itself will negatively impact the entire system (or another part). Let me give you an example from my experience. I worked for a company that implemented a quality improvement program. Every department was asked by leadership to develop a quality "project." The departments recorded their projects' data and sent them monthly to the program coordinator, along with updates on their progress. Senior leaders were ecstatic when one department was asked to present their cost-saving project at a state quality conference. While the department was presenting at the conference, a manager from another department called me to talk about their own project's progress. They explained to me that the department making the presentation had sub-optimized their department, which had to wait longer to finish their work because of improvements in the presenters' cost savings, resulting in decreased productivity. This is an example of why we need to look at interventions from a whole systems organizational point of view. Otherwise, we sub-optimize others, and the business suffers.

LEADERSHIP WHACK-A-MOLE

We conveyed in our introduction to the book, the notion of one organizational action creating unanticipated reactions in other parts of the business by using the analogy of the "whack-a-mole" arcade game. The object of the game is to keep hitting the moles in the head with your mallet until they all go back into their respective holes. The point of the game is that no matter how many times you whack a mole, another one pops up. This represents how problems keep "popping up" again and again because we take a segmental – not a holistic - approach.

Look at your business. Most still maintain the same archaic Industrial Era structures and cultures that keep the organization from changing and prospering. We're still dealing with rigid structures, outdated practices, and limiting cultures. Old leadership and management practices and cultures were key drivers in the recent "Great Resignation," where employees and managers left their jobs in mass - 47 million people in 2021 (Fuller and Kerr, 2022) and 50.5 million in 2022 (Iacurci, 2023).

The good news is that we're finding ways to understand and resolve these problems. Some recent methods are paying off: visioning, purpose, teaming, strategic thinking, Lean Six Sigma, Agile Manufacturing, non-linear organizational structures, experimentation with work protocols, and decentralized decision-making. The question for many companies is how quickly they can adapt to internal and external changes before they hit entropy or dissolution. There are many examples of businesses–large and small–that couldn't adapt and are now shuttered buildings. They didn't look at the whole. They took a segmented approach to change that didn't work.

A note on organizational diagnosis. One of the best holistic models I have worked with in my consulting career is Marvin Weisbord's "Six Box" model (1978). Check out his book in the Bibliography.

LESSONS LEARNED
Open Systems

1. Open Systems interact and exchange materials and information with their external environments.
2. Understanding Open Systems thinking is crucial as our companies face faster and more complex interactions with the environment, evolving customer needs, and important feedback from both internal and external sources.
3. "Systems" are conglomerations of individual parts that interact with each other and the whole system.
4. A change in one part of a system may create changes in other parts of the system and in the whole system itself.
5. Open Systems thinking requires the capability to "see the big picture" of the organization and its markets and external environment.
6. Systems have inputs, throughputs or transformations, and outputs within a boundary. Open systems also have feedback to "control" the system and interaction with their external environments.

LEADERSHIP WHACK-A-MOLE

✱✱✱

Chapter 10

Communication: The Never-Ending Organizational Challenge

Listening Attentively in Spite of the Moles

CHALLENGE QUESTIONS FOR THE READER:

1. In your organization, what was a situation where a management problem was caused by miscommunication?
2. How has information and communication technology changed your ability to communicate in order to achieve organizational outcomes?
3. What has senior leadership done to ensure that teams have the communication skills, support, and accountability needed to adapt to changes?
4. With virtual communication, we lose many signals that assure communication effectiveness. How has this been evident in your remote and hybrid work?
5. How have engagement surveys and communication style assessments helped–facilitate effective communication in your business and/or your team?

In previous chapters and throughout the book, we have referred to an essential element: communication. As we think about the priorities of leadership and managing the outcomes of the enterprise, what comes to mind is the importance of effective communication. Without it, everything comes unglued, and "moles" (i.e., problems) pop up when least expected, creating disharmony and conflict and leading to unwanted outcomes for the business. We provide a few examples in this chapter that demonstrate what effective communication can do for the leader and the organization and the damage ineffective communication can cause.

The purpose of effective communication is to ensure understanding and, most importantly, inspire or cause a desired set of actions to achieve well-defined outcomes. We trust that you will look back on initiatives, challenges, or key actions that went well for you because of effective communication and resulted in outcomes that met or exceeded those of the key constituents and stakeholders of the organization. However, if you are like many leaders, there are examples of times when effective communication was lacking, which resulted in undesirable outcomes and damaged relationships.

When we ask leaders what they believe is the most important element of effective leadership, they often respond with "communication." A saying attributed to Dale Carnegie is that 90 percent of management problems are caused by miscommunication. The reason that leaders rank communication as a top priority is that it affects everything they and the enterprise do.

As we think about communication, we see that it affects almost every aspect of the business. Many associated topics come to mind: team collaboration, productivity, employee engagement, conflict resolution, employee performance feedback and development, organizational alignment, cultural effectiveness, change management, customer service and relations, goal setting, problem-solving, decision-making, workplace safety, and the list could go on and on! The question that perplexes us is, "What is *effective* communication?" The simple answer is: *any communication that results in desired outcomes for the parties involved or affected*. This chapter explores situations that highlight the importance of effective communication. We will assess the results and provide suggestions for improving communication.

RIC'S DIFFICULT EXPERIENCE WITH COMMUNICATION TECHNOLOGY

After finishing my business graduate degree, I assumed my first leadership role at a national company. I was the Manager of Training and Development in a newly formed division of the company. While in my graduate program, I worked with a desktop PC with a program called "Minitab." Outside of my "Minitab" experience, I had minimal experience with computers, voicemail, email, and other forms of office technology. I remember during my onboarding process being shown where I could get pens, legal pads, and flip chart pads to support my work. I was introduced to Jenny in our administrative support group. Jenny was a delightful person; I was fortunate enough that Jenny could decipher my handwriting. This was crucial as I relied on handwritten preparation and typing for written communication, educational materials, and supporting exhibits for my work.

A few months later, I was introduced to the use of personal computers and email communication. While I was somewhat familiar with the use of personal computers, I did not own one at home, and after being introduced to the concept of "emails," I failed to see the value or relevance of it to my work. The communication technology introduced to us could be much more efficiently handled via our office telephones. Our responsible receptionist gladly recorded messages for me whenever someone wanted to speak with me while I was otherwise occupied. I believed that using email technology was unnecessary and a complete waste of my time. Life was good! There were no technology-related emergencies hounding and interrupting my daily routines–no cell phones, no text messages, no "IMs," no backlog of emails in our inboxes, and no complex, tedious shared documents to monitor our daily and weekly progress on our annual goals.

What a different, mind-numbing, and emotion-draining world we now live in! We have access to wonderful new technologies that promise to significantly improve our ability to communicate quickly, access information more readily, and ultimately enhance our individual, team, and corporate productivity. Coming with the new technology is the expectation that we will get the information that we need instantaneously! Wow! How wonderful! Twenty-four hours per day, seven days per week, three hundred and sixty five days per year, we can receive and expect everyone we work with to provide whatever information or access our hearts desire. What that means is that the tyranny of the urgent - instant gratification - has now seized the "free time" we used to savor for family and friends and enjoying life. If you dare to disconnect from this new virtual world for any length of time, you can bet that you will be upsetting countless numbers of coworkers, clients, customers, or even supervisors who are seeking instant information and gratification. Upon returning from a long weekend or vacation, you'll face an overwhelming email inbox, many voicemails, or the hassle of resetting your access. Our expectations can be shattered when technology fails to function, regardless of the reason. Do I sound cynical? In his classic book on communication, *Understanding*

LEADERSHIP WHACK-A-MOLE

Media: The Extensions of Man (1964), Marshall McLuhan introduces the concept of "the medium is the message," where we are shaped by the predominant technologies we use. Communication technology shapes us and our environment, and we must learn to adapt to it (even me!).

Today, I am recounting a technology nightmare I endured a few years ago, which transpired over a six-day period, a few days that seemed like an eternity at the time! During a virtual educational event I was facilitating, my Microsoft Outlook access froze, and it was a nightmare for me. I contacted our corporate IT Help Desk, and the Help Desk technician I talked with advised me to find my home office Wi-Fi password immediately to resolve the issue. Since I couldn't find it right away, I had to disconnect from the Help Desk and the "open ticket" that I had created. After locating the user ID and password for my home internet server, I again contacted the IT Help Desk to resume the online repair. When my call to the Help Desk was answered, I found a different technician on the line. I quickly explained my Outlook access problem to the technician and mentioned the previous technician's solution that required my Wi-Fi credentials. The technician I was speaking with informed me that because I had an "open ticket," I would need to reconnect with the original technician who had been helping me thirty minutes earlier. When I asked if they could transfer me to the original technician, they told me it wasn't possible. I asked if they could give me the original technician's name, but they refused. I inquired about reaching the original technician, and they informed me it could take several days to hear back from them because of the large volume of people needing help. ***CATCH-22!***

Oh, my Lord! The impact of this "impasse" with our IT Help Desk was the cancellation of all scheduled virtual educational sessions, my inability to communicate via the email network, and the frustration among the several hundred leaders who needed the information I was planning to provide. But as I was told, "You are in a large company, and you can *get in line*! My blood pressure was soaring, and my head and heart were both pounding. Within an hour, our Marketing/Communications leader reached out to me via text message to ask me why I was canceling the planned educational sessions, which several hundred of our leaders were anxiously waiting to take part in. Without going into the details of the experience I mentioned above, I informed them I couldn't access the virtual sessions because I was locked out of Outlook. This situation didn't happen just because I was working remotely, contrary to what some might say. The next day, I went to one of our facilities to log in with the hope of resolving the issue, but unfortunately, I found out that I still could not gain access.

The circumstances described in the preceding paragraph affected all forms of personal and organizational communication. Much of what I experienced was not only the direct result of technology not working as it should but also the inflexibility and ineffective design of a Help Desk operation. While I should have been able to resolve the situation by escalating the issue to an IT supervisor, there was no escalation process, and the technicians were not expected to be immediately responsive to customer requests.

When we rely on technology for continued and sustained operations, technological systems will fail, and the ripple effect of both the resulting frustration and stress will multiply rapidly as the failure continues.

Granted, developments in communication technology have improved organizational and personal effectiveness. Faster, more accurate, and complete information can be transmitted in ways that support the coming changes in the workplace: more real-time collaboration in virtual work, greater access to knowledge and information, opportunities to work from anywhere, cost savings, online worker training, and access to global workers. As we gain experience with new communication technology, our frustrations will become the norm.

JEFF ON COMMUNICATION TECHNOLOGY AND ITS IMPLICATIONS

Technology has changed over the decades. At first, I used traditional teaching tools like blackboards and chalk, "overhead" projectors, paper flip charts, and (fruit-smelling) marking pens. The Information Age introduced new technology, including computers, LED projectors, and PowerPoint presentations. Every technology change had a concurrent resistance to its implementation. As Ric identified in his description of his resistance to computers and email, many people are reluctant to convert to newer technologies and are comfortable staying with the current ones.

Reluctance (or inability) to use new technology affects communication. Ric describes the areas of potential impact in the paragraphs above. Later in this chapter, he describes the impacts of virtual and hybrid working on communication. Communicating via computers, tablets, and phones can reduce communication effectiveness (see next paragraph). Communication itself is reduced in virtual or hybrid work structures as fewer people interactions occur. We can only speculate now about the effects Artificial Intelligence (AI) will have on communication in the workplace.

LEADERSHIP WHACK-A-MOLE

With the growth of virtual and hybrid work environments, workers will need to possess excellent communication skills. Computer-based visual interaction loses a great deal of the essential components of effective communication. In a classic study of communication, Dr. Albert Mehrabian at UCLA (1971) found that only 7 percent of effective human communication comes from the actual words used in the communication, 38 percent from voice (tone), and 55 percent from body language. Consequently, when *not* face-to-face, person-to-person, team communication is hampered and can limit the meaning, understanding, or clarity of the discussion. To offset these limitations, employees must be proficient in using words and voice since their body language will not be as apparent online. Effective written, verbal, and visual non-verbal communication skills are necessary to ensure that information and emotions are fully and accurately understood. The elements of true active listening, which enable enhanced empathy and understanding, have become necessities in successful enterprises.

A leader must do more than emphasize communication. It takes a leader who champions and empowers employees to be skilled in the art of communication. *Trust* is necessary for *psychological safety* to become a normal part of how teams and organizations work. This means creating an environment where members feel comfortable sharing their opinions. Communication will become even more important to the "adaptive" business as structural and cultural changes come to life.

Ric's story is not unusual. Communication is often hampered by policies and unwritten rules. In his case, the IT folks had a protocol that dictated their behavior and communication, which negatively impacted their clients. The technology may have been part of the problem, but the policies and protocols of serving the internal customers kept Ric from accomplishing his goal, leaving hundreds of leaders without the information they needed. This is the type of issue that we discussed in previous chapters: Is the performer responsible for the problem? As we looked at in the Performance Management chapter, analyzing the situation would reveal the root causes of the problem was most likely the policy and protocol for handing "trouble tickets." Perhaps the leader of the IT group didn't get feedback about the problem to address and fix it (or they just didn't care–in which case, they may be the root cause). The consequences to the organization can be considerable.

Senior leadership must be sure that teams have the skills, support, and accountability to ensure effective communication. Leaders must establish priorities to effectively communicate and achieve desired outcomes. This will be even more important as change impacts our organizations and more communication flows down to empower teams and individuals. This will help to improve performance, implement new strategies, and create innovation in products and services. Leaders at all levels must manage the communication process. No organizations I am aware of have an internal communication strategy. Most corporate communications training today seems to focus on influencing others rather than communicating for productive conflict and divergence of opinions, which will be the cornerstone of organizational team and project work. Continuous improvement of our communication processes should be as important as improvement of our products and services.

LEADERSHIP WHACK-A-MOLE

RIC ADDRESSES COMMUNICATING "ENGAGEMENT SURVEY" RESULTS

Many large organizations have found it useful to, at least annually, assess the perceptions of their employees through the administration of employee satisfaction or engagement surveys. The purpose of conducting these surveys is to invite the employees to exercise their voices regarding their perceptions of the work environment, the leadership team, and how well the business is supporting the mission, vision, and stated values of the organization. Once results are obtained and analyzed, the leadership team has the responsibility to communicate the results. Leaders then solicit input and involvement in a meaningful action-planning process focused on cultural and organizational improvement. Unfortunately, the organizations conducting these annual surveys often say they want to hear the honest, transparent perceptions of their workforce, but too often, we find that senior leaders overlook the need for follow-up on voiced employee concerns. Senior leaders expect Human Resources (HR) and Organizational Development (OD) leaders to start enterprise-wide communication to address identified issues. Unfortunately, once the HR and OD leaders have completed their work, the action planning process often falls victim to the current ***shiny new objects***" that distract the attention of the senior leaders. By not completely communicating the survey results, employees feel that senior leaders don't care about their concerns or hold anyone responsible for addressing them. The complaints of senior leaders about the workforce's "lack of participation" and enthusiasm in the survey process have been particularly frustrating to me. But what can we expect when the people "on the front lines" perceive that little or nothing has been done in response to their feedback?

LEADERSHIP WHACK-A-MOLE

RIC'S "ENGAGEMENT SURVEY" COMMUNICATION DILEMMA

In one professional role I held during my career, I was responsible for securing, confirming, and accurately disseminating the annual employee engagement and culture survey results to the leadership teams. The organization was a well-respected and highly effective business serving a large consumer base in a geographically dispersed area. For several years, the staff's survey feedback demonstrated a lack of trust in senior leadership. Upon receiving this feedback, the senior leaders decided that they needed to address the lack of trust issue. They decided to enhance the level, frequency, and complexity of the information regularly communicated to the employees. During a series of employee town hall meetings, senior leaders spent most of the time discussing the business' accomplishments – not the survey results or proposed follow-up action. They presented the challenges that senior leadership was having, which left little time for questions from and communicating with the employees. This was a missed opportunity by senior leaders to directly address the trust issue with employees and to provide the information and follow-through action that would help to improve trust, itself.

JEFF OFFERS HIS THOUGHTS ON RIC'S DILEMMA

Much organizational communication–in my experience–is not authentic. Words can distort, manipulate, and conceal in both formal and informal communication. This makes it difficult to have effective communication when the talk intends to conceal one's ends. This is what Ric's employees experienced during the town hall meetings. The senior leaders' words and actions did not change the low trust ratings.

As Ric points out in his example, senior leaders were not "listening" to employees. This was one-way communication, with no opportunity to "close the communication loop" in an actual two-way conversation. As a management consultant, I have seen this scenario play out time after time. Leaders request feedback from employees on organizational matters but don't address the important issues that arise from the results. I have seen the results of the survey "hidden" and not communicated to employees; in another case, the company owner decided that only the "good" survey results would be shared with staff. So, this is not just a communication problem-it's a *leadership problem*.

For change to happen in an organization, employees must have trust in their leaders. Otherwise, change initiatives will probably fail. Given what we have said about the changes that will be required because of the development of technology (for example, artificial intelligence), disruptions in markets, industries, the economy, and a poorly qualified labor pool, leaders must be honest and transparent in their communication. This is the information and mindset that will determine if a business stays competitive or even survives.

RIC'S EXPERIENCE WITH MEETINGS

"Meetings, Bloody Meetings" (Cleese, 1994) is the title of a famous "Monty Python" training film that portrayed corporate meetings as futile efforts to address the issues and challenges of the enterprise. Too often, the communication that occurs before, during, and after the meetings is challenging. Agendas and objectives are not clearly stated or understood. Priorities can be different and conflicting. Critical information is not available or ignored. Emotions can get out of control, and the stress from this can create unacceptable levels of disengagement and frustration. Previously, I described my seven-year-old daughter's innocent response to a friend's question about what her daddy did for work: "he's in charge of meetings and he hates it!" As I reflect on how much time I spent in endless meetings throughout my career, I can confirm that her observations were tragically accurate - so many meetings and so little accomplished! Typically, the results of most of the meetings we attend inspire the participants to pursue differing decisions and actions that trigger unintended consequences in other parts of the organization–more moles (problems) to *whack!* And continued frustration!

Jeff and I worked with a senior consultant at a boutique management consulting firm. His name was Dr. William Thomason. He had a practice model called the "anatomy of an enterprise" that he used in the work he did with clients. At first, we were amused by what we considered to be an overly simplistic perspective on how our clients' businesses operated. However, I have found that as I structured meeting agendas and as I framed how I wanted to pursue a particular organizational communication challenge, Dr. Thomason's anatomy of an enterprise was a consistently sound way to structure my approach.

Following Dr. Thomason's anatomy of an enterprise framework, these meeting guidelines I developed will improve communication and subsequent decision-making and achieve greater outcomes:

1. In collaboration with other key stakeholders, openly communicate with and determine and confirm the purpose and desired results of the planned meeting (verbally and in writing).
2. Clearly outline the meeting objectives, both verbally and in writing.
3. Share the meeting objectives and the agenda with meeting participants and key stakeholders prior to the meeting – including the "ground rules" for the meeting that are consistent with the culture and values of the organization.
4. Incorporate objective and accurate information into the meeting for decision-making purposes – secure such information before the meeting.
5. If the scope of the meeting includes a focus on specific business processes, ensure that the functions/processes being focused on are represented in the meeting by people knowledgeable and credible of those functions and processes.
6. Clearly, accurately, and consistently document decisions made and accountabilities assigned for follow-up and subsequent reporting – establish deadlines and ensure that a communication process for follow-up is in place.
7. Reinforce attendance and participation in the planned meetings with clear consequences for lack of both by the invited participants.

JEFF'S THOUGHTS ABOUT MEETINGS

Someone once said that a meeting is an event where minutes are kept and hours are lost. While we joke about meetings being a waste of time, I see purpose and value in meetings. It's not the meetings that are the problem, but how poorly we design and facilitate them. Dr. Thomason was brilliant at doing both, and his clients produced extraordinary results from their meetings. His structure, as described above by Ric, allowed for a great deal of facilitated communication tied to the meeting's goals.

I keep in mind that meetings can also have "hidden" agendas and dynamics that influence decisions and actions. I was a part of a corporate task force on compensation. The purpose of the group was to review and assess the state of compensation in the corporation. The company's Chief Operating Officer (COO) kicked the meeting off. During their opening, the COO made an off-hand comment that "maybe" every employee (all 100,000 of them) should get a six percent "merit" pay increase at the end of their annual performance cycle. Guess what? We spent much of the project trying to figure out how to give every employee a six percent raise. Even an inadvertent (perhaps joking?) communication by a high-status person can have serious effects on decisions and policies.

RIC DESCRIBES THE ENDLESS MARKET FOR "COMMUNICATION STYLE" ASSESSMENTS

I am convinced that half of the $166 billion-dollar (Westfall, 2019) U.S. market for leadership training (in 2020 alone) is comprised of "communication styles assessments." I enjoy completing, interpreting, and sharing the results of the communication styles. I believe that they help create the "edutaining" environment that, on the surface, participants in training and team-building experiences desire. I have taken and achieved certification in over a dozen different assessment tools. The assessments yield consistent results about my "communication style." I use the *Everything DISC-Work of Leaders* (Wiley, 2011) assessment to augment a variety of learning and coaching experiences. I have found that the instrument helps leaders understand the influence of their communication styles on various aspects of the business.

Some communication styles instruments, while helpful for leaders in understanding themselves and their relationships, have unfortunately been misused in some organizations for making candidate hiring decisions. I worked with a senior executive who used a communication styles instrument to eliminate individuals who didn't meet their ***preferred*** profile for higher-level leadership roles. In fact, if a leader's dominance factor score fell below a certain level, they would show them the exit. What I have found through the years is that no one "style" has a monopoly on leadership. Sometimes, the leadership and communication style should be tailored to match the nature of the business, department, unit, or function. If you have an analytical, calculating, and reserved communication style, you might be a good fit (along with other qualifying criteria) for an Engineering Department. And that individual could be more "comfortable" in that type of environment. Put that type of individual into a rapidly expanding sales organization and the potential fit could be destabilizing.

Individual leaders with cognitive thinking and decision-making abilities understand where their "blind spots" or "discomfort zones" are and will adjust their approaches to avoid misunderstandings or miscommunication. They also understand that a naturally strong communication trait carried to an extreme (i.e., overused and overly leveraged) can easily become a weakness and cause not only miscommunication but potentially destabilizing and destructive conflict. For example, if a leader has a strong preference for thoroughly analyzing detailed data, that preference carried to an extreme can lead to "analysis paralysis" within the business which can keep critical decisions from being made in a timely fashion.

LEADERSHIP WHACK-A-MOLE

JEFF'S FOLLOW-UP TO "COMMUNICATION STYLE" ASSESSMENTS

I also have found various communication style assessments beneficial, particularly in coaching leaders. Recognizing and understanding one's behavioral characteristics in communicating with others can be a growth experience. It helps one to understand others' communication styles and behavior, as well. I used them over my forty years in training and consulting and saw some promising improvements in clients' communication and interaction with others. Most of my engagements in teaching communication styles have been to improve communication – either for individuals or groups. Often, however, such assessments are used for "fun" activities in a workshop or teambuilding event. As mentioned earlier, this is the "edutainer" domain. Yes, seeing the results of your assessment and participating in fun activities has its value – if the purpose is primarily to have fun. That misses the opportunity to help people improve their communication and sometimes their lives.

Changing individual or group communication styles is difficult to do. In addition to well-defined personal styles that one has habituated over many years, the culture of the team or organization affects how people in a group communicate. Change in communication styles, then, requires a considerable planned effort to redefine a culture where every communication style is accepted and utilized to the benefit of the team or business.

LESSONS LEARNED

Communication: The Infinite Organizational Challenge

1. The purpose of communication is to ensure understanding to cause a desired set of actions in support of achieving desired outcomes.
2. Many management problems are caused by miscommunication.
3. Information and communication technology is constantly changing and affects our ability to communicate as well as our organizational outcomes.
4. Building trust into the culture provides "psychological safety" for employees that can lead to a more adaptive organization.
5. Senior leadership must ensure that teams have the communication skills, support, and accountability needed to adapt to changes.
6. Continuous improvement of our communication processes should be as important as improvement of our products and services.
7. With virtual communication, we lose many signals that assure communication effectiveness.

LESSONS LEARNED

Communication: The Infinite Organizational Challenge

8. Engagement surveys and communication styles assessments can facilitate effective communication in the organization and teams.
9. Leaders can build trust by being transparent, honest, and taking action on assessment results.
10. With greater virtual and global work being done, and with the growth of worker diversity, communication effectiveness will be challenged due to language and cultural differences.

✳✳✳

Chapter 11

The Power of Culture

Mole Whacking in Harmony

CHALLENGE QUESTIONS FOR THE READER:

1. What is your definition or description of "culture?"
2. Is your organization's culture "stuck" in old beliefs, behaviors, and values? How does that affect the business' performance and health?
3. How compatible are your personal beliefs, behaviors, and values with your team's and organization's culture?
4. As your workforce diversifies (gig and contract workers, part-time, offshore, gender, language, remote, etc.), how will you adapt your culture to accommodate the diversification?

RIC TALKS ABOUT CULTURE

A simple definition of culture is "the way we do things around here." Organizations often attempt to transform their cultures to improve business outcomes. The true nature of culture is evident in daily communication, rituals, customs, celebrations, and unwritten norms that may be obstacles to achieving those outcomes.

We ask ourselves, "What culture can I best thrive in?" or "Do I fit into the culture I now find myself in?" These are honest, well-intended questions we must answer throughout our careers. In this chapter, we define culture, discuss ways to drive cultural change and explore leadership strategies for high-performing cultures.

CULTURES–NO ONE SIZE AND TYPE FITS ALL

Too often, the leaders and key stakeholders of an organization have their own ideas and opinions about what constitutes an effective culture. Those perceptions can differ from one stakeholder and one senior leader to another. For a business to be successful, it is important for the governing board and senior leadership team to have a common understanding of what they want their culture to reflect. There is no such thing as an "ideal" culture that applies to all organizations. A successful culture is one that reflects the company's vision and values and adjusts to its customers' changing needs. This can be characterized as an "adaptive" culture. A simple model for describing cultures might look something like this on the next page:

Traditional–Highly structured, disciplined, mechanized with little tolerance for deviation– "do it my way or the highway" mentality	**Metrics Focused**– Operational performance measured, tightly structured– meet the numbers - "3 strikes and you're out" mentality.
Collaborative–Relationship focus– "show me you care"– "nice" culture–working together to achieve a goal.	**Innovative**–Loosely structured, supportive of creative, out-of-the-box ideas and initiatives–typically found in start-ups– "involve me" mentality

Table 11.1 Culture Model (adapted from Cameron and Quinn, 2011)

ASSESSING AND DRIVING CULTURAL CHANGE

The culture model in Table 11.1–begs the reader to ask the following questions:

1. Where does my current organization fit in this grid?
2. Where should our organization fit, given what I know about the goals, aspirations, strategies, and values of the company?
3. Should we seek a blend of the cultures represented - a more balanced approach to cultural effectiveness?
4. If my current culture is not what it should be, what actions can move it in that desired direction?
5. How must I change my leadership style to complement the type of culture that our organization should be?

LEADERSHIP WHACK-A-MOLE

(NOTE: If these questions interest you, check out Cameron and Quinn's classic book, *Diagnosing and Changing Organizational Culture* (2011*).* See Bibliography.)

Early in my career, I was intrigued by a growth and adaptability model developed by Larry Greiner in 1972. The Greiner Growth Model is a framework used to understand the different stages of growth that organizations go through. According to Greiner, there are six stages that companies go through, with each stage having its own management challenge.

The Greiner model shows periods of stability and growth, as well as crises caused by management's lack of ability in specific phases of organizational growth. Each crisis brings about a new phase of growth, characterized by a new management style that helps the company to overcome the crisis and continue to grow. With each stage of evolution and the defining associated management styles, changes occur in the culture. Business leaders and analysts use the Greiner model to understand their company's challenges as it grows and evolves. By anticipating and addressing these challenges, organizations can adapt their management and communication styles to meet changing customer needs and foster a positive culture during periods of growth.

Table 11.2 on the following page (adapted from Greiner, ibid.) shows the stages of growth and the challenges faced at each stage, along with a corresponding recommendation for changes in leadership roles and responsibilities. Also emphasized are best leadership practices and behaviors to complement each stage.

LEADERSHIP WHACK-A-MOLE

Stage of Evolution and Crisis Faced	Characterized by	Prioritized Roles/Responsibilities- *Leadership Best Practices/Behaviors*
Leadership/ Direction	Lack of focus, differing perspectives on goals/priorities	Establishing a competitive and compelling vision – *Innovation, Creativity, Conceptual Thinking, Ability to deal with ambiguity, Ability to consider the broad perspective*
Autonomy/ Decision- Making Rights	Functional Roles assuming decision-making rights – much conflict and stress – high turnover	Managing Conflict/Optimizing Structure/Managing Execution – Task/*Project Management, Planning, Resilience, Resourcefulness, Emotional Intelligence, Political Savvy*
Control	Differing practices, miscommunication, need for meetings, continued conflict.	Optimizing Resources – *Humor, Emotional Intelligence, motivating/influencing, coaching/developing others*

Red Tape/ Bureaucracy	Delayed decision-making, missed market opportunities, "bottlenecks"/inefficiencies.	Optimizing Resources – *Humor, Emotional Intelligence, motivating/influencing, coaching/developing others*
Growth Through Collaboration	Apparent need to accelerate decision-making around new market opportunities – emphasis on rapid deployment of resources to new opportunities	Managing an Effective Plan/Maximizing Resources/Investing in Future Leadership – *growth mindset, coaching/developing others, strategic thinking/formulation, global/broad perspective*
Identity	Primary emphasis on organizational identity, long-range (2-5 year) planning, ensuring solid leaders are in place	Establishing a competitive and compelling vision/Cultivating Culture –*Innovation, Creativity, Conceptual Thinking, Ability to deal with ambiguity, Ability to consider the broad perspective, change management, self-confidence, engaging behaviors*

Table 11.2 Greiner Growth Model (adapted from Greiner, 1972)

LEADERSHIP WHACK-A-MOLE

LEADERSHIP STRATEGIES SUPPORTING HIGH-PERFORMANCE CULTURES

The preceding models compel leaders to understand their own strengths and weaknesses. While there are a multitude of leadership assessment tools in the marketplace, most of them do not, by themselves, provide us with a ***holistic*** perspective on our knowledge, skills, abilities, and situations. To effectively lead a business, one must have well-developed conceptual and critical thinking skills. These skills are characterized by a strong ability to articulate issues, challenges, and potential solutions. An effective leader establishes connections between multiple variables in the organization and the external environment, i.e., the ability to "connect the dots!"

Table 11.2 outlines the Greiner model. I have highlighted (in italicized type) those leadership behaviors/best practices that, according to the Eichinger/Pearman model referenced in Chapter 2, are more difficult to develop. As we have cited on multiple occasions throughout the book, our internal and external environments are dynamic and constantly changing. Challenged with the uniqueness of the headwinds facing our businesses, we must make a concerted effort to identify and prioritize the essential roles, responsibilities, and leadership practices that can best drive performance and results. At each stage of evolution, successful leaders will need to possess different strengths and be able to confidently demonstrate leadership behaviors that define the culture needed to meet and exceed the expectations of internal and external customers. For example, in a highly mature, stable organization with a primary emphasis on traditional structure, control, and predictability, task and project management skills complemented by political savvy are critical. However, in an evolving business committed to and primarily focused on continuous improvement and growth, innovation and creativity coupled with a growth mindset will best drive desired performance and success. The Greiner model suggests that most organizations will ultimately face a crisis at each stage of evolution, as outlined in Table 11.2, which will call for potentially dramatic changes in leadership competencies and styles.

In summary, key questions leaders and businesses should regularly ask themselves about culture are:

1. What does a "successful" culture look, feel, and act like, given our own internal expectations and those of our customers?

2. What key roles, responsibilities, and best practice behaviors should we be selecting, developing, recognizing, and reinforcing *at each level* of leadership?

3. How can we, as leaders and as executives, best celebrate and communicate the high performance, or "winning," attributes of our culture to our internal and external customers?

JEFF LOVES CULTURE TALK

Perhaps the most complex and difficult transformation in any organization is changing the culture. There are many models of culture and culture change. We've seen the Greiner model, which looks at the phases of an organization and how it affects the culture.

Cultures develop in various ways. When an organization is young, culture is created primarily by the values, beliefs, leadership styles, problem-solving styles, and behaviors of the founders. These characteristics of the founders permeate the business and shape the behaviors and thinking of the employees. Culture becomes a shared set of the founders' characteristics embodied by most or all of the employees. During the founding and early growth stage, business culture is informal, entrepreneurial, and highly sales-oriented. To enter a new phase of growth, you must develop a more adaptive culture, moving away from the informal organization of the earlier stage.

Employees who did well in the original culture struggle to adjust to a new, more "professional" management style. Some have a difficult time adapting and leave the organization. Even the founder/owner may have a difficult time adjusting, knowing that they are a successful entrepreneur and not a professional manager. I have seen this many times in my consulting work. As Ric mentioned in his discussion of culture, they can–and must–change to adapt to transformations in the external environment or the business strategy. Too often, leaders don't understand the nature and function of their organization's culture or that it will need to adapt to changes. In my consulting career, I've frequently asked business owners and executives to define their company's culture. Too often, their response is, "We're a family culture." This tips me off: they don't understand what culture is and then become confused when they make changes, and the culture resists. Businesses with cultures that are static and don't adapt to today's onslaught of changes will decline and die if their environment becomes dynamic and rapidly changing.

Culture can adapt to changes in the business strategy and external forces. Some believe that culture should not change (especially if the business has been successful). They cling to earlier-stage cultures that were appropriate and effective when the business performed well. They are certain that maintaining the old culture will help them grow even more since it has been successful in the past. As stated before, businesses may fail without adapting their culture.

Some assume that when we use the term "culture change," the entire culture must change. I have seen leaders transitioning to a "customer-centric" or "quality" culture attempt to change all parts of the existing culture at once with a "top-down" approach. However, there are parts of your current culture that are effective and viable. These are the aspects that can remain in place and be integrated into the new culture. Such a procedure requires an assessment of the current culture to determine what aspects of it will align with and enhance the new strategy and culture. A newly envisioned culture can then encompass the vision, values, and behaviors required to make the culture successful. Leaders cannot change a culture without the buy-in of managers and staff. This requires communication with everyone in the organization and putting a formal plan in place to change culture. Culture change takes time, as employees will be skeptical of the change and wonder what the effect will be on them, their jobs, and job security. We must take these and more factors into consideration. Otherwise, human resistance will sink your change effort.

Ric's description of culture as "the way we do things around here" is the most popular one today. To take that a step further, we have to examine *why* we do things that way.

There is a deeper level of understanding for Edgar Schein's (perhaps the foremost expert on organizational culture) model of culture (2019). He describes culture as "a pattern of basic assumptions–invented, discovered, or developed by a group as it learns to cope with its problems." This model comprises three levels, with "artifacts" being the visible aspects of an organization (e.g., employee dress, office layout, etc.); "espoused values" explains why people behave the way they do; and "underlying assumptions"–the unconscious beliefs that define how people see things. According to Schein's model, to change an organization's culture, we need to understand the shared assumptions of the people in the culture. Since these are unconscious, it is difficult to assess these assumptions (or even be aware of them). However, changing a few critical assumptions can lead to behavior changes that can spread throughout the organization.

Ric discussed how adapting culture can lead to better business results and benefit employees, customers, and clients. Culture change can be about engaging your employees in the business and their work. Playing Foosball and end-of-week beer blasts by themselves will not change a culture. A plan is needed to ensure a logical transition. Cultural change entails a great deal of hard and lengthy systematic work. Some cultures may need to adapt more often in hyper-turbulent environments, so we need to regularly assess the culture and its alignment with the organization's vision and changing strategy. When we tie adaptive cultures to business strategies, it becomes a competitive advantage in the marketplace.

Culture connects to everything we discuss in this book–especially employee selection, organizational design, strategic planning, and decision-making. To adopt a customer-centric or innovative strategy, a business will prioritize hiring and developing employees who align with that type of culture. Previously, we discussed the need to implement skills-based performance management, where we hire and deploy people based on the skills they possess to support the expected outcomes of the business. Ideally, our selection processes will enable our businesses to attract candidates with both technical and behavioral skills that are in alignment with the strategy and culture.

Virtual and remote work will affect an organization's culture. Although there is limited information on this topic, maintaining or changing a culture becomes challenging when individuals spend most or all their time away from the office without interacting with peers and managers. The movement toward an "itinerant" workforce will also impact culture. Gig workers, contractors, part-time employees, and outside members of a project may not have opportunities to learn and become immersed in a culture. As itinerant workers, they may have little interest in becoming a part of the culture. Off-shore workers, regular full-time, part-time, or itinerant workers will have cultural differences. These come from their assumptions, values, and behaviors that differ from the hiring organization. I've worked with teams in India, Southeast Asia, and China and seen how difficult it is for them to comprehend American societal and business cultures. In addition, language differences add another dimension to the difficulty, not only with foreign languages. For example, I worked with a colleague from England who used terms that were acceptable in British culture but offensive in American culture.

Culture is also a strong determinant of employee retention and attrition. Cultures promoting purpose, values, development, autonomy, safety, leadership, and respect improve employee retention. Businesses that neglect these qualities or foster toxic cultures will have a higher rate of employee turnover. Leaders must consider the cultural elements that employees desire. Most leaders I've worked with believe it's up to those at the top to establish the right culture for the company. While this is typically true, it is also imperative to help employees see their fit and adapt to the culture.

Otherwise, what a way to create employee mistrust and resistance.
Whack!

Companies can no longer leave the business of culture creation and sustainability to Human Resources or Organizational Development. The organization cannot achieve culture adoption solely through motivational wall posters and a four-hour presentation. Think back to my example of the business owner who posted the company vision and values on the wall and asked all employees to sign the paper to show agreement with the vision and values. The only signatures on the paper were the senior leaders–not one employee signed. Cultural adoption and change require more than words, pizza parties, and motivational posters. They begin with *commitment from the top* and active modeling of the behaviors that visibly show "living" the vision and values–that is, "walking the talk."

In the new world of work, employees often bring their own visions and values to a company, which may or may not match the company's. If a fit doesn't exist, the workers may become disillusioned, or their performance may suffer. Large numbers of employees cannot feasibly take part in creating or revising a vision. There would not be a common vision among them. A vision is the creation of the enterprise's founder, owner, or senior leadership group. We can, however, help employees to align their personal vision and values with the organization's.

Culture plays a critical role in organizational health and performance, as well as in adapting to internal and external changes. Companies in dynamic environments and competitive industries and markets will do well to ensure that culture supports adaptation and change rather than resistance that results in dire consequences for the business.

LESSONS LEARNED

The Power of Culture

1. We need to reflect on whether we "fit" into our organization's culture.
2. There are differing models and theories of culture with varied elements in them.
3. Organizations grow into new developmental stages throughout the course of their existence. Culture will change at certain stages and we must be prepared to adapt (e.g. newly-founded entrepreneurial vs. bureaucracy).
4. Some leaders don't want their cultures to change. They wish to keep the culture that made them successful regardless of the dysfunction it may create in the organization.
5. Diversification of the workforce may change culture due to the differing values and beliefs new workers bring to the organization.

Chapter 12
Adding Value and Getting Results

Putting the Moles to Rest, Once and For All

CHALLENGE QUESTIONS FOR THE READER:

1. What can you do to make yourself a more effective leader?
2. Can you name and celebrate those people in your career whom you have coached and guided to live successful and productive lives?
3. What makes you feel hopeful about your future as a leader?

At the beginning of the book, we said that there were twelve obstacles to effective leadership. We've been through eleven chapters and you may be wondering, how is this chapter an obstacle? The obstacle we see in "Adding Value and Getting Results" is just that – the difficulties in both adding value to the organization and achieving results. These can be difficult to do, so we see them as potential barriers to successful leadership. In this chapter, Ric will take you through a series of exemplary questions and ideas for you to ponder and compare with your own current leadership situation. Enjoy the chapter!

LEADERSHIP WHACK-A-MOLE

RIC PUTS THE MOLES TO REST – SUNSET BEACH, NORTH CAROLINA

"Have I earned the respect and admiration of those people who have contributed so much to my life and my career over the past fifty years?" I ask myself. There were many people, colleagues, leaders, and personal friends who helped me through challenging times with the hope and expectation that I would make the most of my life and career. As I prepare to retire, I ask myself with some hesitancy, "Did I give it my best?" I doubt I am alone with the nagging sense of remorse that periodically compels many of us to look back and question the decisions and choices we made along the way. In the opening paragraph of the introduction to this book, I reflected on a state of mind that I could not sustain over the next twenty-two years. I lingered too long following career paths that robbed me and those whom I was close to - the joy that all of us should strive for and deserve in life.

I am not perfect, nor are those leaders and aspiring leaders who might read this book. As we conveyed several times throughout the preceding eleven chapters, we hope that the insights, questions, and other resources provided will enable the readers to maximize the impact they make in their leadership roles and seize the joy that can come with their engagement in and commitment to well-balanced personal and professional lives.

It is the responsibility of leaders to create a clear vision, align resources, and coordinate efforts to achieve results. While this expectation might seem simple, what we have discovered is that deep into the complexity of work life, maintaining vigilance and oversight of these key leadership "musts" can be challenging. This chapter provides guidance on decision-making and leadership practices for success in the short and long term.

Key questions to ask ourselves as they relate to the leadership charge outlined above are:

Regarding creating a vision, to what degree am I...

1. Open to new ideas and expectations of my team?
2. Aware of the environmental factors that impact my area of responsibility?
3. Assuming responsibility for taking risks?
4. Voicing and communicating the direction of my team(s) with other organizational stakeholders?
5. Reaching out to outside "experts" to help define our vision?
6. Testing or validating with the key stakeholders of the business the assumptions made supporting the vision created for my assigned team(s)?

Regarding ensuring team alignment, integration, and coordination, to what extent am I...

1. Providing full explanations and transparency with my team(s)?
2. Having a structured and consistent communication approach with my team and key stakeholders?
3. Encouraging ongoing dialogue and open communication with my team(s) and key stakeholders?
4. Open to the ongoing thoughts, suggestions, and inputs from my team(s) and key stakeholders?
5. Dedicating time and energy to providing inspiration and encouragement to my team(s) and key stakeholders?

LEADERSHIP WHACK-A-MOLE

Regarding follow-through and execution, to what extent am I...

1. Confirming my personal motivation and drive to ensure full execution of our plan/vision?
2. Holding myself accountable for driving the vision's implementation and acceptance across the company?
3. Carefully planning and paying attention to the details necessary for the successful implementation of my goals and priorities?
4. Conducting detailed analysis as necessary to ensure accuracy and alignment with the expected outcomes of the vision and supporting plan(s)?
5. Monitoring and providing feedback to my team during the execution of plans?
6. Acknowledging and recognizing the individuals and teams involved in the successful implementation of the vision and supporting plan(s)?

In one of my Organization Development leadership roles, I facilitated a program to orient new leaders to the organization. This session introduced leaders to the business' primary expectations of them and offered resources for their unique challenges. Besides offering some straightforward "tips for success," I recommended asking themselves the following immediate questions to their respective managing directors or executives.

1. What are this year's primary goals and expectations for my division, department, unit, or function?
2. Which goals do I need to achieve before the year ends? (no more than 3)

3. To ensure the successful attainment of these goals, which resources (budget, people, information, tools) are currently at my disposal or still need to be obtained?

4. What key processes need improvement in order for me to be successful in my new role? What can I do now to address any concerns?

5. Who are my direct reports? What concerns exist regarding these individuals? What current and future actions are planned or need to be planned for these people?

6. Can I provide an update on the productivity of our unit, department, division, and organization? Where might I have inefficient or ineffective functions, processes, or people?

7. What is my current budget? How am I performing against that budget? What actions do I need to take to stay on budget?

8. Which regulatory and compliance gaps or issues require attention? Where and when can I review the expectations and standards for compliance in my area(s) of responsibility?

And I convey and reinforce for the new leaders the simple "rules of engagement" to be successful...

1. Support The Organization's Mission, Vision, and Values
2. Be Present and Punctual
3. Be Responsive (one business day expectation to respond internally)
4. Demonstrate Respect and Dignity
5. Follow Policy
6. Follow Through–Keep Your Promises
7. Support, Enable, Empower, and Ensure the Capabilities of Your Staff
8. Speak Up–Challenge with Respect
9. Grow Your Skills and Knowledge.

LEADERSHIP WHACK-A-MOLE

IN CLOSING...

Our book underscores the importance of prioritizing, deciding, and acting in accordance with personal and organizational values. In the opening paragraph of this chapter, Ric reflected on what we often discover - that sometimes we may not have been true to our personal values, and we bear a sense of regret or disappointment. We believe that no leader is perfect. But if we remain true to ourselves and focus on our employees and customers, we will have done worthy things.

Jeff stressed the importance of working holistically and within systems and to be thoughtful about implementing segmented solutions to problems (i.e., Flavor of the Month). Looking at the "big picture" and the individual parts of the business and how they all affect one another will give you a new perspective on managing and growing an organization. Change is inevitable. We never anticipated so much change so quickly, but we must learn to adapt in many new ways. Be innovative in coming up with those ways. The future awaits us. Let's prepare now.

One source has described *Walk the Talk* (1995) as a book that demonstrates the importance of aligning actions with words, emphasizing the value of integrity, authenticity, and leading by example in business environments. It offers insights into effective leadership practices and the significance of staying true to one's values to achieve desired results. We couldn't agree more.

We've come to the end of ***Leadership Whack-A-Mole***. We hope that we've communicated the idea that leadership isn't only about offering others vision and direction. It's also about learning about ourselves as people. We trust you found some practical and proven ideas and strategies that will inspire you to grow in your leadership journey and make a positive impact on the people and communities you serve.

***

About Ric Shriver

Ric Shriver has over 40 years of progressive Human Resources and Organizational Development experience in the Healthcare, Hospitality, and Consulting industries.

Growing up in West Des Moines, Iowa, Ric recognized early in his life that he had a natural inclination and ability to recognize and pursue vocational and recreational paths that often reflected the "less traveled" paths in life. His vocational paths started early in his life with growing, cultivating, and selling to his Iowa neighbors' various fruits and vegetables. He ultimately graduated from gardening and promoted himself to the role of a "paperboy" for the Des Moines Register & Tribune, which he enthusiastically filled through his junior high years. While Ric dreamed of becoming a varsity football, basketball, or baseball player in high school, he recognized that his real strength was any sport that required less natural hand-eye coordination and more mental, cardiac, and emotional strength. Consequently, Ric became a long-distance runner. Through his high school years and after moving with his family from Iowa to North Carolina, Ric's desire and ability to distance his rivals became obvious. He won the North Carolina State 2-mile championship in 1971 and was offered an athletic scholarship for cross-country and track to Appalachian State University.

After his sophomore year and without a clear conviction for his ultimate career, Ric chose to take an alternative and more challenging path by enlisting in the U.S. Navy. Ric continued to train and compete during his enlistment, which landed him an active role on the Military Cross-Country and Track Team, a role that required him to be able to travel on the weekends to various sites in the U.S. and Europe to represent his country in international competition. For Ric to live up to the Navy's athletic expectations, the Navy assigned him to a "Personnel Department" role on the remote base in North Africa where he had been stationed. Ric fell in love with "Personnel", and upon returning to college following his enlistment, knew exactly where his career would be – Human Resources!

Following his graduation from undergraduate school at Appalachian State University, Ric pursued an initial Human Resources (HR) specialization in Compensation while working for a community-based health system in Roanoke, Virginia. Within a few short years, Ric developed a keen interest in Leadership and Organizational Development (L&OD). Knowing that for him to rise to a desired level in the L&OD field, he would need to have a graduate degree, Ric returned to his alma mater to complete a formal graduate program with a focus on Business Management, Business Education, and Industrial Psychology.

Upon completion of his graduate studies, Ric went to work for a nationally recognized management company in their management development department. Ric was ultimately promoted to the role of Manager, Executive, and Organizational Development in that company. After a corporate restructuring, Ric moved back into the not-for-profit world, where he progressed from a managerial role to becoming a senior HR Officer for a reputable organization. Ric ultimately moved into the senior HR Officer role with a national management contract services company, then to an expanded role with a large national, for-profit enterprise as the senior HR Officer for the company's largest division. While residing in Florida, Ric was appointed to Florida's Workforce Board (now CareerSource Florida) by Governor Rick Scott. His affiliation with the Workforce

LEADERSHIP WHACK-A-MOLE

Board refueled his interest in Leadership & Organizational Development and ultimately paved the way for him to return to both a national and a regional L & OD role within his company and subsequently with a competing organization in Virginia.

Ric's credentials include holding a Master's degree in Business and Economics from Appalachian State University, earning his Senior Professional in Human Resources (SPHR) in 1996, being certified as a professional facilitator by DDI, Edge Learning, Miller-Heimann Sales Training, Just Culture, Inc., TalentTelligent, Inc., and Wiley Publishing (DISC). In his role on the Florida Workforce Board (CareerSource Florida), he was named Chair of the Global Talent & Competitiveness Council and as the Board Liaison for the Florida Healthcare Initiative.

Personally, Ric was an accomplished distance runner in college, winning Junior National and Southern Conference Champion titles in several distance running events. Ric finished in the top 100 at the Boston Marathon in 1979. He is also a U.S. Navy Veteran, having served as both a Radioman and a Personnel "Yeoman" for the 6th Fleet while stationed in North Africa in the early 70s.

Ric most recently served as the Corporate Director, Learning & Organizational Development for a health system in Virginia. He and his wife Janet will be retiring to the North Carolina Coast later this year, where they will devote full time to their shared passions of art and writing, three beautiful daughters, and two handsome grandsons.

To learn more about Leadership Whack-A-Mole, view the website at www.leadershipwhackamole.com.

To contact Ric, email ric@leadershipwhackamole.com

***

About Jeff Fierstein

Jeff Fierstein, co-author of *Leadership Whack-A-Mole*, is the Founder and Principal of **GOAL ACHIEVE! LLC**, a global management consultancy. Based in Phoenix, Arizona, Jeff worked with leaders to improve their individual, team, and organizational performance through strategic planning and operational execution, process and quality improvement, team effectiveness, executive and manager coaching, talent development, and performance management.

Jeff held internal mid-level leadership roles specializing in performance and talent management in Fortune 40 to small entrepreneurial companies. He has more than 40 years of experience in creating and teaching performance-based learning as a certified practitioner in Criterion Referenced Instruction (CRI) and Instructional Module Development (IMD). As an experienced Human Resources (HR) practitioner, Jeff has a background in HR Management, Training, and Organization Development.

As a consultant, Jeff has over 40 years of progressive Human Resources, Organizational Development, and General Management Consulting experience in 35 industries. Through direct coaching, training, and consulting, he directly impacted over 33,000 professionals in 13 countries throughout North America, Asia, and Europe. People have acknowledged Jeff for his holistic and systems approach to addressing and solving the many challenges his clients faced. He has provided services for Honeywell, Bank of America, Best Western Hotels, the American Heart Association, U.S. Department of Veterans Affairs, AT&T, Motorola, Times-Mirror

LEADERSHIP WHACK-A-MOLE

Cable, IPQE Limited (Hong Kong), U.S. Postal Service, Take Charge America, U-Haul International, Make-A-Wish, and 100+ organizations.

Attending the University of Illinois, Jeff holds two Master's degrees and a Professional Certificate in Human Resource Development, and earned the designation of Senior Professional in Human Resources (SPHR). His articles have appeared in *Management Review*, *Training and Development*, *Performance & Instruction*, *Executive Education in America*, *Phoenix Business Journal*, *Making Training Pay Off on the Job*, and *Training*. He served as President of the National Healthcare Chapter and the Arizona Chapter of the International Society for Performance Improvement (ISPI).

As an Adjunct Professor in Ottawa University's Master's in Human Resources program for 13 years, Jeff taught a broad range of graduate courses in Human Resources and Organization Development. He served as Advisor for the student chapter of the Society for Human Resource Management (SHRM) and as an instructor in Ottawa's international Human Resource Master's program based in Hong Kong.

Now retired in Arizona with his wife Linda, Jeff enjoys periodic speaking and coaching engagements while spending most of his time with his wife, three grown children, grandchildren, and rescue dogs. A native of Chicago, Jeff is a devoted Bears (American football) and Cubs (baseball) fan.

To learn more about Leadership Whack-A-Mole, view the website at www.leadershipwhackamole.com.

To contact Jeff, email jeff@leadershipwhackamole.com

Bibliography

INTRODUCTION

Peck, M. Scott. *The Road Less Traveled*. New York: Simon and Shuster, 1978.

CHAPTER 1

Adizes, Ichak. *Corporate Lifecycles*. Saddle River, New Jersey: Prentice Hall, 1989.

Bennis, Warren. *On Becoming a Leader*. New York: Basic Books, 1989.

Fayol, Henri. *General and Industrial Management*. London: Pitman, 1949.

Greiner, Larry E. "Greiner Model of Organizational Evolution." Harvard Business Review, 1998.

Hogan, R., G. Curphy, R. Kaiser, and T. Chamorro-Premuzic. *Hogan Talent Development* Tulsa, OK: Hogan Assessments, 2018.

CHAPTER 2

Collins, Jim. *Good to Great: Why Some Companies Make the Leap...and Others Don't*. New York: Harper Business, 2001.

Eichinger, Robert, Roger Pearman, Kathryn Spinelli, and Garrick Throckmorton. *TalentTelligence*. Winston-Salem, NC: TalentTelligent.

Green Dot Aviation. "How did this plane end up MILES off course? American965."
https://www.youtube.com/watch?v=TEHna_Rre78.

McCall, Morgan W. Jr., Michael M. Lombardo, and Ann M. Morrison. *The Lessons of Experience: How Successful Executives Develop on the Job*. Los Angeles: Free Press, 1988.

Peters, Thomas J., and Robert H. Waterman Jr. *In Search of Excellence: Lessons from America's Best Run Companies.* New York: Harper and Row, 1982.

Westfall, Chris. "Leadership Development is a $366 Billion Industry: Here's Why Most Programs Don't Work," *Forbes*, June, 2019.

CHAPTER 3

Hoonan, Suzanne. "Weekly Insights." Hoonan & Associates, October 2023 (Quote published with the permission of Suzanne Hoonan,R.N., M.A)

Mowad, Bob. *Increasing Human Effectiveness*. Annapolis, MD: Legacy Business Cultures, 2006.

Pink, Daniel. *Drive: The Surprising Truth About What Motivates Us*. New York: Riverhead Hardcover, 2009.

Vroom, Victor H. *Work, and Motivation*. San Francisco: Jossey-Bass, 1964.

CHAPTER 4

Bersin, Josh. "Introducing the Learning & Development SuperClass," Josh Bersin, October 25, 2023 (https://joshbersin.com/2023/10/introducing-the-learning-development-superclass/).

Deming, W. Edwards. *Out of the Crisis*. Cambridge, MA: MIT Center for Advanced Engineering Study, 1986.

Fierstein, Jeff. "Let's Get Rid of the Training Department," *Training*, June 1988. Used with permission of Training magazine.

Fierstein, Jeff. *Appraise the Performance System…Not the Performer*. Unpublished paper, 1999.

Fierstein, Jeff. *The Performance Planner*. Unpublished paper, 1994.

Gilbert, Thomas. "A Question of Performance. Part 1: The PROBE Model." *Training and Development Journal*, 1982 (Vol. 36, No. 9, pp. 20-22, 24-30). Used with permission.

Hsieh, Tony. *Delivering Happiness: A Path to Profits, Passion, and Purpose.* New York: Hachette Book Group, Inc., 2010.

Iacoviello, Marco." How Does Artificial Intelligence Create New Jobs?" *Forbes*, July 26, 2023.

Ishikawa, Kaoru. *Introduction to Quality Control*. Oxfordshire, UK: Taylor and Francis, 1990.

Just Culture Algorithm, The Just Culture Company, Ft. Lauderdale, Florida, 2019

Lencioni, Patrick. *The Five Dysfunctions of a Team: A Leadership Fable*. San Francisco: Jossey-Bass, 2002.

Likert, Rensis. "A technique for the measurement of attitudes." *Archives of Psychology*, 1932.

Mager, Robert F. *Making Instruction Work*. Atlanta: Center for Effective Performance, 1988.

Robertson, Brian J. *Holacracy: The New Management System for a Rapidly Changing World*. New York: Henry Holt and Company, 2015.

Rummler, Geary A. and Alan P. Brache. *Improving Performance: How to Manage the White Space on the Organization Chart*. San Francisco: Jossey-Bass, 1995.

U.S. Bureau of Labor Statistics. "Job Openings and Labor Turnover Summary," Economic News Release, January 30, 2024.

Whitmore, Paul. "When We Teach, What Gets Learned? Today's Crisis in Corporate Training," *Performance Improvement Quarterly*, Vol. 3, Issue 1, 1990.

CHAPTER 5

Drucker, Peter. "Insights Hub." Rotman School of Management. May, 2021.

Rummler, Geary A. *Serious Performance Consulting According to Rummler*. Detroit, MI: Pfeiffer, 2007.

U.S. Bureau of Labor Statistics. Labor Force Statistics from the Current Population Survey. January, 2024.

CHAPTER 6

Purushothaman, Deepa and Lisen Stromberg. "Leaders Stop Rewarding Toxic Rock Stars," *Harvard Business Review*, April 2022.

CHAPTER 7

Lencioni, Patrick. *The Five Dysfunctions of a Team: A Leadership Fable*. San Francisco: Jossey-Bass, 2002.

Thomas, Kenneth W., and Ralph H. Kilmann. *Thomas-Kilmann Conflict Mode Instrument*. Mountain View, CA: Consulting Psychologists Press, 1974.

CHAPTER 8

Beer, Michael, Russell Eisenstat, and Bert Spector. "Why Change Programs Don't Produce Change," *Harvard Business Review*, November-December, 1990.

Brown, Shona and Kathleen Eisenhardt. "The Art of Continuous Change: Linking Complexity Theory and Time-Paced Evolution in Relentlessly Shifting Organizations," *Administrative Science Quarterly*, March 1997.

Collins, James, and Jerry Porras. *Built to Last: Successful Habits of Visionary Companies*. New York: Harper Business, 1994.

D'Aveni, Richard. "The Aftermath of Organizational Decline: A Longitudinal Study of the Strategic and Managerial Characteristics of Declining Firms." *Academy of Management Journal*, 1989.

Fierstein, Jeff. *How Organizations Really Change: A Research Model*. (Unpublished paper), 1999.

Fitz-Enz, Jac. *The 8 Practices of Exceptional Companies*. New York: AMACOM, 1997.

Johnson, Homer, *Characteristics of Sustained Competitive Success in Organizations*. In the 1997 Annual: Volume 2, Detroit, MI: Pfeiffer 1997.

Kanter, Rosabeth Moss. *The Change Masters*. Seattle, WA: Touchstone, 1983.

Kanter, Rosabeth Moss, Barry Stein, and Todd Jick. *The Challenge of Organizational Change*. Los Angeles: Free Press, 1992.

Kilmann, Ralph, et. al. *Corporate Transformation*. San Francisco: Jossey-Bass, 1988.

Kotter, John and James Heskett. *Corporate Culture and Performance*. Los Angeles: The Free Press, 1992.

Kotter, John, "Leading Change: Why Transformation Efforts Fail," Harvard Business Review, March-April, 1995.

Kotter, John P. and Holger Rathgeber. *Our Iceberg Is Melting: Changing and Succeeding Under Any Conditions*. New York: St. Martin's Press, 2006.

Price Waterhouse. *Better Change*. Irwin, 1995.

Quinn, James Brian. *Strategies For Change: Logical Incrementalism*. Homewood, IL: Richard D. Irwin, 1980.

Robinson, Alan and Sam Stern. *Corporate Creativity*. Berrett-Kohler, 1998.

Schaffer, Robert, and Harvey Thomson. "Successful Change Programs Begin with Results," Harvard Business Review, January-February, 1992.

Schein. Edgar. *Organizational Culture and Leadership. (5th ed)*. Hoboken, New Jersey: Wiley, 2019.

Shriver, Ric. "I.M.P.A.C.T. Model," Unpublished paper, 2021.

CHAPTER 9

Bersin, Josh. "Introducing the Learning & Development SuperClass," Josh Bersin, October 25, 2023 (https://joshbersin.com/2023/10/introducing-the-learning-development-superclass/).

Fuller, Joseph, and William Kerr. "The Great Resignation Didn't Start with the Pandemic," Harvard Business Review, March 23, 2022.

Iacurci, Greg. "2022 was the Real Year of the Great Resignation," CNBC, February 1, 2023.

Weisbord, Marvin R. *Organizational Diagnosis: A Workbook of Theory and Practice*. Reading, MA: Addison-Wesley, 1978.

Wolf, Jason A. *Transforming the Future of Healthcare*. Nashville, TN: The Beryl Institute, 2024.

CHAPTER 10

Cleese, John, Anthony Jay, and Peter Robinson. *Meetings, Bloody Meetings* (Video). London: Video Arts, 1994.

Everything DISC® Work of Leaders. New York: Wiley, 2011.

McLuhan, Marshall. *Understanding Media: The Extensions of Man.* New York: McGraw-Hill, 1964.

Mehrabian, Albert. *Silent Messages*. Belmont, CA: Wadsworth, 1971.

Thomason William. *The Anatomy of an Enterprise*. Unpublished paper. Nashville, TN: William Thomason & Associates, 1987

CHAPTER 11

Cameron Kim S. and Robert E. Quinn. *Diagnosing and Changing Organizational Culture (3rd edition)*. San Francisco: Jossey-Bass (Wiley), 2011.

Greiner, Larry E. "Evolution and Revolution as Organizations Grow" Harvard Business Review 50, no. 4 (1972): 37-46

Schein. Edgar. *Organizational Culture and Leadership* (5th Ed.). New York: Wiley, 2019.

CHAPTER 12

Harvey, Eric Lee and, Steve Ventura. *Walk the Talk: --and Get the Results You Want.* Bedford, TX: The Walk The Talk Company, 2003.

References

CHAPTER 1 – LEADERSHIP

Brown, Sara. "15 Assumptions Leaders Should Reconsider," *MIT Sloan*, May 10, 2022.

Bryant, Adam. "What's Most Needed from Managers Now," *The New York Times*, June 6, 2022.

Cappelli, Peter. "Stop Overengineering People Management," *Harvard Business Review*, September-October, 2020.

Center for Creative Leadership. "Purpose in Leadership: Why & How," February 5, 2024.

Charan, Ram. *What the CEO Wants You to Know*. New York: Crown Business, 2001.

Connors, Christopher D. *Emotional Intelligence for the Modern Leader: A Guide to Cultivating Effective Leadership and Organizations*. Emeryville, CA: Rockridge Press May 19, 2020.

Denning, Steve. "The Reinvention of Management: Part 3: From Controller to Enabler," January 19, 2011. https://stevedenning.typepad.com/steve_denning/2011/01/the-reinvention-of-management-part-3-from-controller-to-enabler.html

Denning, Steve. "The Death - and Reinvention - of Management: Part 1," November 17, 2010. https://stevedenning.typepad.com/steve_denning/2010/11/the-death-and-reinvention-of-management-a-draft-synthesis.html

DiGangi, Julia. "The Anxious Micromanager," *Harvard Business Review*, September-October, 2023.

Edmondson, Amy, Sujin Jang, and Tiziana Casciaro. "Cross-Silo Leadership," *Harvard Business Review*, May-June, 2019.

Field, Emily, Bryan Hancock, and Bill Schaninger. "Don't Eliminate Your Middle Managers," *Harvard Business Review*, July-August, 2023.

Harvey, Eric, and Alexander Lucia. *Walk the Talk*. Dallas, TX: Performance Publishing Company, 1995.

Heifetz, Ronald and Donald L. Laurie. "The Work of Leadership," *Harvard Business Review*, December 2001.

Irwin, Tim. "When Leaders Go Off Track: Executive Derailers," Development Dimensions International, June 2005.

Kanter, Rosabeth Moss. "The New Managerial Work," *Harvard Business Review*, November-December, 1989.

Kotter, John P. "What Leaders Really Do," *Harvard Business Review*, December 2001.

Meshanko, Paul. *The Respect Effect*. New York: McGraw-Hill Education, 2013.

Pistrui, Joseph and Dimo Dimov. "The Role of a Manager Has to Change in 5 Key Ways," *Harvard Business Review*, October 26, 2018.

Schoemaker, J.H., Steve Krupp, and Samantha Howland. "Strategic Leadership: The Essential Skills," *Harvard Business Review*, January-February, 2013.

Straw, Julie, Mark Scullard, Susie Kukkonen, and Barry Davis. *The Work of Leaders*. San Francisco, CA: John Wiley & Sons, 2013.

"The Best Leadership Books of All Time," Soundview, Inc., 2022.

Watkins, Michael D. "How Managers Become Leaders," *Harvard Business Review*, June 2012.

Wigert, Ben and Heather Barrett. "The Manager Squeeze: How the New Workplace is Testing Team Leaders," *Gallup Workplace*, September 6, 2023.

CHAPTER 2 – LEADERSHIP DEVELOPMENT

Bersin, Josh. "Companies Have Been Neglecting Their Leadership, And It Shows," The Josh Bersin Company, November 6, 2023.

Cahill, Alice, Laura Quinn, and Lawrence McEvoy, II. "Are You Getting the Best Out of Your Executive Team?" Center for Creative Leadership, 2017.

Camilleri, Vanessa A. "The Future's Top Workplaces Will Rely on Manager Development," *Workplace*, November 13, 2020.

Center for Creative Leadership. "15 Experiences That Help You Learn to Lead," December 1, 2023.

Chamorro-Premuzic, Tomas. "5 Ways to Develop Talent for an Unpredictable Future," *Harvard Business Review*, October 9, 2023.

Charan, Ram, Steve Drotter, and Jim Noel. *The Leadership Pipeline*, San Francisco, CA: Jossey-Bass/John Wiley & Sons, 2011.

Church, Zach. "Writing a New Leadership Playbook," *MIT Sloan Management Review*, March 3, 2020.

Ferris, Karen. "We Have a Leadership Crisis–Identifying and Developing Talent," LinkedIn, May 9, 2023.

Ferris, Karen. "7 Factors Affecting the Impact of Organizational Leadership Development," Center for Creative Leadership, January 7, 2022.

Gurdjian, Pierre, Thomas Halbeisen, and Kevin Lane. "Why Leadership Development Programs Fail," *McKinsey Quarterly*, January 2014.

Landry, Lauren. "Why Emotional Intelligence is Important in Leadership," *Harvard Business Review*, April 3, 2019.

Leroy, Hannes, Moran Anisman-Razin, and Jim Detert. "Leadership Development Is Failing Us. Here's How to Fix It." *MIT Sloan Management Review*, December 06, 2023.

Leinwand, Paul, Mahadeva Matt Mani, and Blair Sheppard. "Reinventing Your Leadership Team," *Harvard Business Review*, January-February 2022.

Martinez, Freddie. "The 7 Most In-Demand Skills Driving the Leadership Gap," *Big Think*, September 5, 2023.

McCauley, Cindy. "What's the 70-20-10 Framework?" Center For Creative Leadership, April 24, 2022.

Ratanjee, Vibhas. "Why Managers Need Leadership Development Too," *Workplace*, January 8, 2021.

Taylor, Bill. "If Humility is So Important, Why Are Leaders So Arrogant?" *Harvard Business Review*, October 15, 2018.

Thorton, Chris. "Are You Failing to Prepare the Next Generation of C-Suite Leaders?" LinkedIn, May 30, 2023.

CHAPTER 3 - MOTIVATION

Covey, Stephen M.R., and David Kasperson. *Trust and Inspire: How Truly Great Leaders Unleash Greatness in Others*. San Francisco, CA: Berrett-Koehler Publishers. April 4, 2023.

Deci, Edward L., and Richard Flaste. *Why We Do What We Do: Understanding Self-Motivation*. London: Penguin. August 1, 1996.

Donahue, Wesley E. *Boosting Employee Motivation and Engagement: A Competency-Based Approach to Increasing Employee Performance by Focusing on the Work Climate*. San Francisco, CA: Berrett-Koehler Publishers. February 14, 2022.

Doshi, Neel, and Lindsay McGregor. *Primed to Perform*. New York: Harper Business, 2015.

Fowler, Susan. *Why Motivating People Doesn't Work…and What Does, Second Edition: More Breakthroughs for Leading, Energizing, and Engaging*. San Francisco, CA: Berrett-Koehler Publishers. May 16, 2023.

Haasen, Adolf and Gordon F. Shea. *A Better Place to Work*. New York: AMA Management Briefings, 1997.

Haasen, Adolf and Gordon F. Shea. *New Corporate Cultures That Motivate*. Westport, CT: Praeger, 2003.

Kerr, Steven (Editor). *Ultimate Rewards: What Really Motivates People to Achieve*. Cambridge, MA: A Harvard Business Review Book. 1997.

Latham, Gary P. *Work Motivation: History, Theory, Research, and Practice*. Thousand Oaks, CA: Sage Publications, 2007.

McGregor, Lindsay, and Neel Doshi. "How to Keep Your Team Motivated, Remotely," *Harvard Business Review*, April 9, 2020.

Neuhauser, Peg, Ray Bender, and Kirk Stromberg, *I Should Be Burnt Out by Now*. Mississauga, Ontario, Canada: John Wiley and Sons, Ltd., 2004.

Sinek, Simon. *Start With Why: How Great Leaders Inspire Everyone to Take Action*. London: Portfolio/Penguin, 2009.

Thomas, Kenneth W. *Intrinsic Motivation at Work*. San Francisco, CA: Berrett-Koehler Publishers. 2000.

CHAPTER 4 – PERFORMANCE MANAGEMENT

Buckingham, Marcus and Ashley Goodall. "Reinventing Performance Management," *Harvard Business Review*, April 2015.

Cantrell, Sue. "Navigating the End of Jobs," Deloitte, January 9, 2023.

Cappelli, Peter and Anna Tavis. "The Performance Management Revolution," *Harvard Business Review*, October 2016.

Cappelli, Peter and Anna Tavis. "HR Goes Agile," *Harvard Business Review*, March-April, 2018.

Culture Amp. "5 Steps for Transforming Your Performance Management Process," https://www.cultureamp.com/resources/ebooks/5-steps-for-transforming-your-performance-management-process.

Culture Amp. "HR Guide to Continuous Performance Management," https://cultureamp.com, November 8, 2022.

Davar, Zubin. "The #1 Reason Why People Leave Companies: How Performance Management Can Stop It," *Performance Insights*, June 20, 2023.

Gratton, Lynda. "Predictions for the Workplace of 2025, Revisited." *MIT Sloan Review*, January 16, 2024.

Hatfield, Steve. "Activating the Future of Workplace," Deloitte, January 9, 2023.

Heger, Brian. "Linking Talent Strategy with Business Strategy," Talent Edge Weekly, September 7, 2023.

Martin, Jean, and Conrad Schmidt. "How To Keep Your Top Talent," *Harvard Business Review*, May 2010.

Sethi, Bhushan, Blair Sheppard, and Nicole Wakefield. "Meet the Four Forces Shaping Your Workforce Strategy," *Strategy + Business*, April 12, 2022.

DEFINE THE JOB

Crocker, Alia, Rob Cross, and Heidi K. Gardner. "How to Make Sure Agile Teams Can Work Together." *Harvard Business Review*, May 15, 2018.

Nieto-Rodreguez, Antonio. "A New Approach to Writing Job Descriptions," *Harvard Business Review*, October 6, 2023.

Gardner, Heidi K., and Ivan Matviak. "Performance Management Shouldn't Kill Collaboration," *Harvard Business Review*, September-October 2022.

Groysberg, Boris, Eric Lin, Abhijit Naik, and Sascha L. Schmidt. "Identify Critical Roles to Improve Performance," *MIT Sloan Management Review*, August 14, 2023.

Jesuthasan, Ravin and John W. Boudreau. *Work Without Jobs*. Cambridge, MA: The MIT Press, 2022.

Moorman, Christine, and Katie Hinkfuss. "Managing the Cultural Pitfalls of Hybrid Work," *MIT Sloan*, May 2, 2023.

Smith, Tyrone. "It's Time to Rethink Job Descriptions for the Digital Era," *Harvard Business Review*, December 8, 2021.

The Josh Bersin Company. "HR Predictions for 2024: Imperatives for The Year Ahead," The Josh Bersin Company, 2024. https://joshbersin.com/josh-bersins-predictions-for-2024.

Westerman, George. "Rethinking Assumptions About How Employees Work" (podcast). Solarwinds Techpod, October 27, 2021. https://orangematter.solarwinds.com/2021/11/02/george-westerman-building-the-culture-for-digital-transformation-solarwinds-techpod-052.

Wickman, Gino. *Traction*. Dallas, TX: BenBella, 2011.

SELECT THE RIGHT TALENT

Bradberry, Simon, and Bruce Norton. "Unlock the Potential of a Skills-Based Organization," *MIT Sloan Management Review*, October 12, 2023.

Davis, Kathleen. "LinkedIn Exec Reveals Exactly How AI Is Changing Hiring and Recruiting," LinkedIn, October 30, 2023.

Fuller, Joseph, Nithya Vaduganathan, Allison Bailey, and Manjari Raman. "40 Ideas to Shake Up Your Hiring Process," *Harvard Business Review*, January 16, 2023.

Gratton, Lynda. "Redesigning How We Work," *Harvard Business Review*, March-April, 2023.

Groysberg, Boris, Nitin Nohria, and Claudio Fernandez-Araoz. "The Definitive Guide to Recruiting in Good Times and Bad," *Harvard Business Review*, May 2009.

Knight, Rebecca. "7 Practical Ways to Reduce Bias in Your Hiring Process," *Harvard Business Review*, June 12, 2017.

McCord, Patty. "How to Hire: Chances are You're Doing It All Wrong," *Harvard Business Review*, January-February 2018.

Menkes, Justin. "Hiring for Smarts," *Harvard Business Review*, November, 2005.

Poundstone, William. "Beware the Interview Inquisition," *Harvard Business Review*, May 2003.

DEVELOP THE TALENT

Cantrell, Sue. "The Skills-Based Organization: A New Operating Model for Work and the Workforce," *Deloitte Insights*, September 8, 2022.

Chamorro-Premuzic, Tomas. "5 Ways to Develop Talent for an Unpredictable Future," *Harvard Business Review*, October 09, 2023.

Doty, Elizabeth. "How to Help Your Employees Own Your Strategy," *Strategy + Business*, Summer, 2020.

Glaveski, Steve. "Where Companies Go Wrong with Learning and Development," *Harvard Business Review*, October 2, 2019.

Rath, Tom. *Strengths Finder 2.0.* Gallup, NM: Gallup Press, 2007.

Senge, Peter. The Fifth Discipline. New York, NY: Currency Doubleday/Bantam Doubleday, 1990.

Warner, Todd. "Corporate Learning Programs Need to Consider Context, Not Just Skills," *Harvard Business Review*, November 10, 2017.

Tamayo, Jorge, Leila Doumi, Sagar Goel, Orsolya Kovacs-Ondrejkovic, and Raffaella Sadun. "Reskilling in the Age of AI," *Harvard Business Review*, September-October, 2023.

Whitmore, Paul. *How to Make Smart Decisions About Training: Save Money, Time, and Frustration*. Atlanta, GA: Center for Effective Performance, 2001.

ASSESS AND DOCUMENT TALENT

Brown, Jeremy. "5 Dirty Secrets of Performance Reviews," *Strategy + Business*, August 29, 2023.

Chamorro-Premuzic, Tomas. "4 Reasons Talented Employees Don't Reach Their Potential," *Harvard Business Review*, March 18, 2019.

Davar, Zubin. "The #1 Reason Why People Leave Companies: How Performance Management Can Stop It," *Performance Insights*, June 20, 2023.

Doran, George T. "There's a S.M.A.R.T. Way to Write Management's Goals and Objectives," *Management Review*, 1981.

Kenny, Graham. "Fixing Performance Appraisal Is About More than Ditching Annual Reviews," *Harvard Business Review*, February 2, 2016.

Levinson, Harry. "Appraisal of What Performance?" *Harvard Business Review*, July 1976.

Murray, David. "Feedback Examples: How to Give Great Performance Feedback," *Harvard Business Review*, July 27, 2023.

Owens, Lisa M.D. "Fixing Performance Reviews for Good," SHRM Labs, May 8, 2023.

Rock, David, Josh Davis, and Beth Jones. "Kill Your Performance Ratings," *Strategy + Business*, August 8, 2014.

Tabrizi, Benham. "Why the Performance Review is Dying Out– Including at Companies Like Apple and Microsoft," *Fast Company*, August 24, 2023.

COACHING

Boyatzis, Richard E., Melvin L. Smith, and Ellen Van Oosten. *Helping People Change: Coaching with Compassion for Lifelong Learning and Growth*. Cambridge, MA: Harvard Business Review Press, September 10, 2019.

Campbell, Bill. *Trillion Dollar Coach: The Leadership Handbook of Silicon Valley's Bill Campbell*. New York: Harper Business, April 16, 2019.

Ibarra, Herminia and Anne Scoular. "The Leader as Coach," *Harvard Business Review*, November-December, 2019.

Pereira, Nitin. "Managers Can't Be Great Coaches All by Themselves," *Harvard Business Review*, May-June, 2018.

Phillips, Kim Walsh, et al. *Behind the Scenes: Secrets from the Top Coaches, Experts, and Consultants*. Glen Rock, PA: Year of the Book Press, November 1, 2019.

Stanier, Michael Bungay. *The Coaching Habit*. Box of Crayons Press, February 29, 2016.

DEALING WITH PERFORMANCE PROBLEMS

Brock, David "The Secret to Accelerating Performance: What Winning Companies Do Differently," *Forbes*, September 21, 2023.

Chandler, M. Tamra. *How Performance Management is Killing Performance — and What to Do About It*. Oakland, CA: Berrett-Koehler Publishers, 2016.

Falcone, Paul. "101 Tough Conversations to Have with Employees: A Manager's Guide to Addressing Performance, Conduct, and Discipline Challenges," AMACOM, April 8, 2009.

Kinley, Nik, and Shlomo Ben-Hur. *Changing Employee Behavior*. London: Palgrave Macmillan, 2015.

Kirkpatrick, Donald L. *Improving Employee Performance Through Appraisal and Coaching*. New York: AMACOM, January 25, 2006.

CHAPTER 5 - CUSTOMERS

Bliss, Jeanne. *Chief Customer Officer 2.0: How to Build Your Customer-Driven Growth Engine.* New York: Wiley, June 5, 2015.

Carlzon, Jan. *Moments of Truth*. New York: HarperCollins, 1987.

Denning, Steve. "The Reinvention of Management: Part 2: How Do You Delight the Client?" *Strategy + Business*, January 18, 2011.

Dixon, Matthew, Nick Toman, and Rick DeLisi. *The Effortless Experience: Conquering the New Battleground for Customer Loyalty*. New York: Penguin Random House, September 12, 2013.

Feldman, Stuart. "Keeping the Customer Satisfied – Inside and Out," *Management Review*, November 1991.

Frei, Frances and Anne Morriss. *Uncommon Service: How to Win by Putting Customers at the Core of Your Business.* Cambridge, MA: Harvard Business Review Press, February 7, 2012.

Johnson, Michael D. and Anders Gustafsson. *Improving Customer Satisfaction, Loyalty, and Profit: An Integrated Measurement and Management System.* San Francisco: Jossey-Bass, August 1, 2000.

Hsieh, Tony. *Delivering Happiness: A Path to Profits, Passion, and Purpose.* New York: Grand Central Publishing, June 7, 2010.

Mehta, Nick, Dan Steinman, and Lincoln Murphy. *Customer Success: How Innovative Companies Are Reducing Churn and Growing Recurring Revenue.* New York: Wiley, February 2016.

Reichheld, Fred. *Winning on Purpose: The Unbeatable Strategy of Loving Customers.* Harvard Business Review Press, November 30, 2021.

Reichheld, Frederick F. and Rob Markey. *The Ultimate Question 2.0: How Net Promoter Companies Thrive in a Customer-Driven World.* Cambridge, MA: Harvard Business Press, 2011.

Zhou, Alice, Isabel Aguirre, and Matt Egol. "The Inside-Out Approach to Customer-Centricity," *Strategy + Business*, February 16, 2023.

CHAPTER 6 – TOXIC PEOPLE

Carucci, Ron. "3 Ways Senior Leaders Create a Toxic Culture," *Harvard Business Review*, May 1, 2018.

LEADERSHIP WHACK-A-MOLE

Cohen, Arianne. "Psychologists Have Finally Figured Out Why Your Toxic Colleagues Climb to the Top At Work," No Desk, March 18, 2020. https://nodesk.co/articles/psychologists-have-finally-figured-out-why-your-toxic-colleagues-climb-to-the-top-at-work/

Gallo, Amy. "How to Manage a Toxic Employee," *Harvard Business Review*, October 3, 2016.

Kets de Vries, Manfred F.R. "Coaching the Toxic Leader," *Harvard Business Review*, April 2014.

McClean, Shawn, Stephen H. Courtright, Troy A. Smith, and Junhyok Yim. "Stop Making Excuses for Toxic Bosses," *Harvard Business Review*, January 19, 2021.

McGinn, Dan. "Toxic Workplaces" (podcast). *Harvard Business Review*, May 3, 2018. https://hbr.org/podcast/2018/05/toxic-workplaces

McKee, Annie. "Keep Your Company's Toxic Culture from Infecting Your Team," *Harvard Business Review*, April 29, 2019.

Offermann, Lynn. "When Followers Become Toxic," *Harvard Business Review*, January 2004.

Pavlou, Christina. "How to Identify and Address 'Toxic Employees," *Workplace*, April 18, 2020

https://resources.workable.com/stories-and-insights/toxic-employees

Porath, Christine, and Christine Pearson. "How Toxic Colleagues Corrode Performance, *Harvard Business Review*, April 2009.

Priesemuth, Manuela. "Time's Up for Toxic Workplaces," *Harvard Business Review*, June 19, 2020.

Purushothaman, Deepa and Lisen Stromberg. "Leaders, Stop Rewarding Toxic Rock Stars," *Harvard Business Review*, April 20, 2022.

Templer, Klaus J. "Why Do Toxic People Get Promoted? For the Same Reason, Humble People Do: Political Skill," *Harvard Business Review*, July 10, 2018.

Time Doctor. "10 Common Toxic Workplace Behaviors and How to Prevent Them," November 18, 2020. https://www.timedoctor.com/blog/toxic-workplace-behaviors/

Sull, Donald, Charles Sull, and Ben Zweig. "Toxic Culture Is Driving the Great Resignation," *World Economic Forum's Strategic Intelligence*, January 11, 2022.

Westerman, George. "Rethinking Assumptions About How Employees Work" (podcast). SolarWinds TechPod, November 2, 2021.

CHAPTER 7 - CONFLICT

Blank, Sam. *Managing Organizational Conflict*. Jefferson, NC: McFarland Books, 2020.

Gallo, Amy. *HBR Guide to Dealing with Conflict*. Cambridge, MA: Harvard Business Review Press, 2017.

Gallo, Amy. "Why We Should Be Disagreeing More at Work," *Harvard Business Review*, January 3, 2018.

Guttman, Howard M. *When Goliaths Clash.* Mt. Arlington, NJ: Guttman Development, 2008.

Harper, Shaun. "Why Business Leaders are Pulling the Plug on DEI," *Forbes,* July 18, 2018.

Nicotera, Anne Maydan. *Conflict and Organizations.* Albany, NY: State University of New York Press, October, 1995.

Rahim, M. Afzalur. *Managing Conflict in Organizations.* Abingdon, UK: Taylor & Francis, 2023.

Stone, Douglas, Bruce Patton, and Sheila Heen. *Difficult Conversations.* London: Penguin Publishing Group, August 22, 2023.

Zheng, Lily. *DEI Deconstructed.* Oakland, CA: Berrett-Koehler Publishers, 2022.

CHAPTER 8 - CHANGE

Andersen, Erika. "Change is Hard. Here's How to Make It Less Painful," *Harvard Business Review*, April 7, 2022.

Ashkenas, Ron. "How to Avoid the Churn That Comes with Agility," *Harvard Business Review*, September 20, 2023.

Borkan, Brad. "The Power of Incremental Momentum," *Strategy + Business*, December 15, 2022.

Boyatzis, Richard E., Melvin Smith, and Ellen Van Oosten. "Coaching for Change," *Harvard Business Review*, September-October, 2019.

LEADERSHIP WHACK-A-MOLE

Carucci, Ron. "How Leaders Get in the Way of Organizational Change," *Harvard Business Review*, April 30, 2021.

Charan, Ram. "What Defines a Successful Organization?" *Harvard Business Review*, September 19, 2022.

Clayton, Sarah Jensen. "An Agile Approach to Change Management," *Harvard Business Review*, January 11, 2021.

Gordon, Jason. "What is Logical Incrementalism?" The Business Professor, LLC, August 21, 2023 .https://thebusinessprofessor.com/en_US/management-leadership-organizational-behavior/logical-incrementalism-explained.

Kavanaugh, Jeff, and Rafee Tarafdar. "Break Down Change Management into Small Steps," *Harvard Business Review*, May 3, 2021.

Kegan, Robert and Lisa Lahey. "The Real Reason People Won't Change," *Harvard Business Review*, November 2001

Knowles, Jonathan, B. Tom Hunsaker, and Melanie Hughes. "The Role of Culture in Enabling Change," Walden Dissertations, October 4, 2023.

Kotter, John P. and Leonard A Schlesinger. "Choosing Strategies for Change," *Harvard Business Review*, July-August, 2008.

Muhdi, Louise. "How to jump-start innovation and organizational change," *Strategy + Business*, January 12, 2022.

Olson, Andrea Belk. "Old Formulas Won't Help You Solve Today's Business Problems," *Harvard Business Review*, October 23, 2023.

LEADERSHIP WHACK-A-MOLE

PwC. "Reinvention Momentum is Building for CEOs," PwC on LinkedIn, February 3, 2024. https://www.linkedin.com/posts/pwc_for-ceos-reinvention-momentum-is-building-activity-7159311962768637952-Sruo[1]

Quinn, James Brian. "Strategic Change: 'Logical Incrementalism,'" *Sloan Management Review*, Fall, 1978.

Rowland, Deborah, Michael Thorley, and Nicole Brauckmann. "The Most Successful Approaches to Leading Organizational Change," *Harvard Business Review*, April 20, 2023.

Satell, Greg. "Want People to Embrace Transformation? Allow Them to Own the Change," *Harvard Business Review*, October 2, 2023.

Schaffer, Robert H. "All Management is Change Management," *Harvard Business Review*, October 26, 2017.

Schwartz, Tony. "Leaders Focus Too Much on Changing Policies, and Not Enough on Changing Minds," *Harvard Business Review*, June 25, 2018.

Sirkin, Harold L., Perry Keenan, and Alan Jackson. "The Hard Side of Change Management," *Harvard Business Review*, October, 2005.

White, Andrew, Michael Wheelock, Adam Canwell, and Michael Smets. "6 Key Levers of a Successful Organizational Transformation," In "The Leadership Agenda: CEO – PwC," PWC, May 10, 2023.

CHAPTER 9 – OPEN SYSTEMS

Clark, Dorie. *The Long Game: How to Be a Long-Term Thinker in a Short-Term World*. Cambridge, MA: Harvard Business Review Press, September 21, 2021.

Clark, Dorie. "The Long Game: "Your Strategic Thinking Self-Assessment," dorieclark.com/thelonggame/

Clark, Dorie. "If Strategy Is So Important, Why Don't We Make Time for It," *Harvard Business Review*, June 21, 2018.

Favaro, Ken. "Why Popular Strategies Always Fade," *Strategy + Business*, May 25, 2016.

Fierstein, Jeff. "Don't Plan Strategically, Manage Strategically," LinkedIn, May 17, 2018.

Haines, Stephen. "Strategic and Systems Thinking: From Chaos to Complexity to Elegant Simplicity," Centre for Strategic Management, 2005.

Krippendorff, Kaihan and Claudio Garcia. "Is Organizational Hierarchy Getting in the Way of Innovation?" *Harvard Business Review*, September 12, 2023.

Lancefield, David, and Daniel Gross. "The Clear Sky Strategy," *Strategy + Business*, July 15, 2020.

Leinwand, Paul and Joachim Rotering. "How to Excel at Both Strategy and Execution," *Harvard Business Review*, November 17, 2017.

LEADERSHIP WHACK-A-MOLE

Lencioni, Patrick. *The Advantage*. San Francisco, CA: Jossey-Bass, 2012.

Mankins, Michael C. "Making Strategy Development Matter," *Harvard Management Update*, February 27, 2008.

Markovitz, Daniel. *"Productivity Is About Your Systems, Not Your People," Harvard Business Review*, January 5, 2021.

Porter, Michael E. "What Is Strategy?" *Harvard Business Review*, November-December, 1996.

Praslova, Ludmila N. "Today's Most Critical Workplace Challenges Are About Systems," *Harvard Business Review*, January 10, 2023.

Razzouk, Rim and Valerie Shute. "What Is Design Thinking and Why Is It Important?"*Review of Educational Research*, September 1, 2012.

Reeves, Martin, Simon Levin, Thomas Fink, and Ania Levina. "Taming Complexity," *Harvard Business Review*, January-February, 2020.

Si, Haijian, Christoph Loch, and Stelios Kavadias. "A New Approach to Strategic Innovation," *Harvard Business Review*, September-October, 2023.

Sørensen, Jesper B. and Glenn R. Carroll. "Practicing Strategy in an Uncertain World," *Strategy + Business*, Summer, 2021.

Van Durme, Yves. "Leading In a Boundaryless World: Reshaping the Way That You Lead and Influence Others," *Deloitte Insights*, January 9, 2023.

Webb, Amy. "How to Do Strategic Planning Like a Futurist," *Harvard Business Review*, July 30, 2019.

Wiita, Nathan and Orla Leonard. "How the Most Successful Teams Bridge the Strategy-Execution Gap," *Harvard Business Review*, November 23, 2017.

CHAPTER 10 – COMMUNICATION

"100 Best Communication Books of All Time," Shortform, 2021.

Anonymous. *Modern Theories of Organizational Communication.* Washington, D.C.: International Communication Association, 2004.

Heath, Chip, and Dan Heath. *Made to Stick: Why Some Ideas Survive, and Others Die.* New York: Random House: January 2, 2007.

Jones, Elizabeth, Bernadette Watson, John Gardner, and Cindy Gallois. "Organizational Communication: Challenges for the New Century," International Communication Association, January 10, 2006.

Lehman, Carol M. and Debbie D. DuFrene. *Business Communication.* Mason, OH: Cengage Learning, February 19, 2010.

Myers, Karen K. and Kamyab Sadaghiani. "Millennials in the Workplace: A Communication Perspective on Millennials' Organizational Relationships and Performance," University of California, 2010.

Shribman, Michael. "A Guide for Mastering the Art of Business Communication," *Forbes*, Nov 20, 2023.

Various Authors. *HBR's 10 Must Reads on Communication*. Cambridge, MA: Harvard Business Review Press, April 2, 2013.

Williamson, Blair. "10 Books to Improve Business Communication Skills," *Nextiva Blog*, November 11, 2022

CHAPTER 11 - CULTURE

Bailey, Catherine, Catherine Tilley, and Anna Lelia Sandoghdar. "What Makes a Great Corporate Purpose Statement," *Harvard Business Review*, September 11, 2023.

Corbetta, Luna, and Margo Stokum. "Culture: Transformation's Invisible Enabler," *Strategy + Business*, July 12, 2022.

Deal, Terrence and Allen Kennedy. *Corporate Cultures*. Redwood City, CA: Addison-Wesley Publishing Company, 1982.

Daimler, Melissa. *ReCulturing: Design Your Company Culture to Connect with Strategy and Purpose for Lasting Success.* New York: McGraw-Hill, 2022.

Hugander, Per. "Take a Skills-Based Approach to Culture Change," *MIT Sloan Management Review*, May 22, 2023.

Lancefield, David. "How to Develop an Intrapreneurial Culture," *Strategy + Business*, August 9, 2023.

Lancefield, David. "Mastering the Connection Between Strategy and Culture," *Strategy + Business*, Issue 106, Spring 2022.

Pedersen, Carsten Lund. "Cracking the Culture Code for Successful Digital Transformation," *MIT Sloan Management Review*, April 06, 2022.

Ratanjee, Vibhas, and Ed O'Boyle. "Diagnosing a Broken Culture – and What to Do About It," Gallup, August 4, 2023.

Ready, Douglas. "Does Your Company Suffer from Broken Culture Syndrome?" *MIT Sloan*, January 10, 2022.

Somers, Meredith. "3 common myths about work culture," *Harvard Business Review*, May 24, 2022.

Sull, Donald, and Charles Sull. "How to Fix a Toxic Culture," *MIT Sloan Management Review*, September 28, 2022.

Sull, Donald and Charles Sull. "10 Things Your Corporate Culture Needs to Get Right," MIT Sloan Management Review, September 16, 2021.

Watkinson, Allan, and Rohit Kar. "Organizational Culture: What Leaders Need to Know," Gallup, March 24, 2023.

CHAPTER 12 – GETTING RESULTS

Burris, Ethan. "How to Sell Your Ideas up the Chain of Command," *Harvard Business Review*, January-February 2022.

Doerr, John. *Measure What Matters*. London: Portfolio/Penguin, 2018.

Goldratt, Eliyahu M. *The Goal* (4th Revised Edition). Great Barrington, MA: North River Press, 2014.

Redmon, Marsha. "Presenting to the Big Dogs: How to Hold Your Own in Executives Ranks," *Harvard Business Review*, October 2001.

Rhoades, Ann. *Built on Values*. San Francisco: Jossey-Bass, 2011.

Smith, Nicole D., and Angela Cheng-Cimini. "How to Become More Visible at Work," Harvard Business School Publishing, August 18, 2023.